CREATING CAPABILITIES

CREATING CAPABILITIES

The Human Development Approach

Martha C. Nussbaum

THE BELKNAP PRESS OF
HARVARD UNIVERSITY PRESS
Cambridge, Massachusetts, and London, England

Printed in the United States of America

First Harvard University Press paperback edition, 2013

Library of Congress Cataloging-in-Publication Data
Nussbaum, Martha Craven, 1947–
Creating capabilities: the human
development approach / Martha C. Nussbaum.
p.   cm.
Includes bibliographical references (p.   ) and index.
ISBN 978-0-674-05054-9 (cloth : alk. paper)
ISBN 978-0-674-07235-0 (pbk.)
1. Social justice.   2. Economic development.
3. Women's rights.   I. Title.
HM671.N868   2011
303.3′72—dc22   2010044834

To all the members of the
Human Development and Capability Association

Contents

PREFACE

For a long time, economists, policy-makers, and bureaucrats who work on the problems of the world's poorer nations told people a story that distorted human experience. Their dominant models asserted that the quality of life in a nation was improving when, and only when, Gross Domestic Product (GDP) per capita was increasing. This crude measure gave high marks to countries that contained alarming inequalities, countries in which a large proportion of people were not enjoying the fruits of a nation's overall economic improvement. Because countries respond to public rankings that affect their international reputation, the crude approach encouraged them to work for economic growth alone, without attending to the living standard of their poorer inhabitants, and without addressing issues such as health and education, which typically do not improve with economic growth.

This model persists. Although it is most firmly entrenched in standard analyses of the achievements of "developing countries"— as in the practice of development economics and in agencies associated with development, such as the International Monetary Fund (IMF) and the World Bank—it is also widely used to think about richer nations and what it means for them to "develop" or to improve their quality of life. (All countries are "developing countries," although that phrase is sometimes used to refer to poorer countries: every nation has a lot of room for improvement in delivering an adequate quality of life to all its people.) Since these nations also contain large inequalities, the approach generates similar distortions in them.

Today there is a new theoretical paradigm in the development and policy world. Known as the "Human Development" approach, and also as the "Capability Approach" or "Capabilities Approach," it begins with a very simple question: What are people actually able to do and to be? What real opportunities are available to them? This question, though simple, is also complex, since the quality of a human life involves multiple elements whose relationship to one another needs close study. Indeed, one of the appealing features of the new approach is its complexity: it appears well equipped to respond to the complexities of human life and human striving. After all, the question it poses is one that people ask themselves often in their daily lives.

This new paradigm has had increasing impact on international agencies discussing welfare, from the World Bank to the United Nations Development Programme (UNDP). Through the influence of the Human Development Reports published each year since 1990 by the United Nations Human Development Report Office, it also now affects most contemporary nations, which have been inspired to produce their own capability-based studies of the well-being of different regions and groups in their own societies. Few nations today do not regularly produce such a report. (Even the United States joined the group in 2008.) There are also regional reports, such as the *Arab Human Development Report*. In addition, the Human Development and Capability Association (HDCA), with membership of approximately 700 drawn from 80 countries, promotes high-quality research across a broad range of topics where the human development and capability approaches have made and can make significant contributions. Most recently, the paradigm has had a major influence on the Sarkozy Commission Report on the measurement of economic performance and social progress.

The increasingly influential Capabilities Approach has been expounded primarily in dense articles and books for specialists. Repeatedly, general readers and instructors in undergraduate courses have lamented the lack of a more accessible book on the topic. This book aims to fill that gap, making the key elements of the approach clear and helping people assess it against its rivals. Above all, it attempts to situate the approach in the narrative context of human lives, showing how it makes a difference to what policy-makers notice in these lives and, hence, to the ability of policy to construct meaningful interventions that show respect for and empower real people, rather than simply reflecting the biases of intellectual elites.

Improving people's quality of life requires wise policy choices and dedicated action on the part of many individuals. It may seem unnecessary, then, to write a theoretical book on the topic, however immersed in narrative detail. Theories, however, are a large part of our world, framing the way issues are seen, shaping perceptions of salience, and thus slanting debate toward certain policies rather than others. Wise activists have all too little influence in the corridors of power. Because the dominant theories that have historically guided policy choice in this area are deeply mistaken, as I shall argue, they have steered development policy toward choices that are wrong from the point of view of widely shared human values (such as respect for equality and respect for dignity). We need a counter-theory to challenge these entrenched but misguided theories, if we want to move policy choice in the right direction. Such a counter-theory should articulate the world of development in new ways, showing us a different picture of what our priorities should be. The Capabilities Approach is the counter-theory we need, in an era of urgent human problems and unjustifiable human inequalities.

CREATING CAPABILITIES

I

A WOMAN SEEKING JUSTICE

All over the world people are struggling for lives that
are worthy of their human dignity. Leaders of countries often focus on national economic growth alone, but their people, meanwhile, are striving for something different: meaningful lives for
themselves. Increased GDP has not always made a difference to the
quality of people's lives, and reports of national prosperity are not
likely to console those whose existence is marked by inequality and
deprivation. Such people need theoretical approaches that can aid
their struggles, or at least provoke public debate by drawing attention to them; they do not need approaches that keep these struggles
hidden or muffle discussion and criticism. As the late Mahbub ul
Haq, the Pakistani economist who inaugurated the Human Development Reports of the United Nations Development Programme,
wrote in the first of those reports, in 1990: "The real wealth of a nation is its people. And the purpose of development is to create an
enabling environment for people to enjoy long, healthy, and creative
lives. This simple but powerful truth is too often forgotten in the
pursuit of material and financial wealth." According to Haq, development economics needs a new theoretical approach if it is to respond to people's most urgent problems.

GDP - Gross Domestic Product

Consider Vasanti, a small woman in her early thirties who lives in Ahmedabad, a large city in the state of Gujarat, in northwestern India. Vasanti's husband was a gambler and an alcoholic. He used the household money to get drunk. When that money was gone, he got a vasectomy to take advantage of the cash incentive that Gujarat's government offered to encourage sterilization. So Vasanti had no children to help her, a huge liability, given the fact that a childless woman is more vulnerable to domestic violence. Eventually, as her husband became more abusive, she left him and returned to her own family.

Poor parents (or siblings, if the parents have died) are often unwilling to take back a child who has been married, especially a female child who took a dowry with her. Accepting the child back into the home means another mouth to feed and a new set of anxieties. In Vasanti's case, a divorce would prove costly because her husband was unwilling to grant one. It was her good fortune, then, that her family was willing to help her. Many women in her position end up on the street, with no alternative but sex work. Vasanti's father, who used to make Singer sewing machine parts, had died, but her brothers were running an auto parts business in what was once his shop. Using one of his old machines, and living in the shop itself, Vasanti earned a small income making eyeholes for the hooks on sari tops. Meanwhile, her brothers gave her a loan to get another machine, one that rolls the edges of the sari. She took the money, but she didn't like being dependent on her siblings—they were married and had children, and their support could end at any time.

Vasanti then discovered the Self-Employed Women's Organization (SEWA), a pathbreaking nongovernmental organization (NGO) in Ahmedabad that works with poor women. Founded by the internationally acclaimed activist Ela Bhatt, SEWA had by that time helped more than 50,000 members, with programs including microcredit, education, health care, and a labor union. Unlike some other Indian states, Gujarat has followed a growth-oriented agenda without devoting many resources to the needs of its poorest inhabitants. Government programs that might have helped Vasanti—legal aid, health care, credit, education—were not to be found. It was her good luck that one of the best NGOs in India happened to be in her own backyard.

With the help of SEWA, Vasanti got a bank loan of her own and paid back her brothers. (SEWA, which began as a humble credit union, now operates a bank in an impressive office building in downtown Ahmedabad. All the officers and employees of the bank are women, many of them former beneficiaries of SEWA's programs.) By the time I met her, several years later, she had paid back almost all the SEWA loan itself. She was also eligible to enroll in SEWA's educational programs, where she was planning to learn to read and write and to acquire the skills necessary to promote greater social and economic independence and political participation. With the help of her friend Kokila, she was actively involved in combating domestic violence in her community. This friendship would have been very unlikely but for SEWA; Vasanti, though poor, is from the high Brahmin caste, and Kokila is from one of the lower castes. Though still all too evident in society in general, divisions along lines of caste and religion are anathema in the Indian women's movement.

What theoretical approach could direct attention to the most significant features of Vasanti's situation, promote an adequate analysis of it, and make pertinent recommendations for action? Suppose for a moment that we were interested not in economic or political theory but just in people: what would we notice and consider salient about Vasanti's story?

First we would probably notice how small Vasanti is, and we could initially take this as evidence of poor nutrition in childhood. Poor families are often forced to feed all their children poorly, but we would want to ask about how her brothers fared. Evidence abounds that girls are less well nourished than boys and less often taken to the doctor in childhood when ill. Why? Because girls have fewer employment opportunities than boys and thus seem less important to the well-being of the entire family. The work they do in the home does not bring in money, so it is easy to overlook its economic importance. Moreover, in northern and western India girls move away from the family when they marry, taking a dowry with them. They are thus more expensive than boys, and parents often wonder why they should spend their resources on girls who won't be around to support them in their old age. The mortality of second daughters in northern and western India is notoriously high. So Vasanti's nutritional deficiency is a result not just of poverty but also of gender discrimination.

Unequal laws of property and inheritance contribute to the predicament of India's daughters, and anyone thinking about Vasanti's life must consider the role they have played in her situation. The religion-based systems of personal law that have existed in India since Independence govern property and inheritance as well as family law. All the systems institutionalize large inequalities for women. Until 1986, for example, Christian women inherited only one-fourth of what sons inherited, a custom that surely contributes to defining the worth of a daughter's life as less than that of a son's. Hindu women, too, have suffered inequalities under the Hindu property code; they attained equal shares in agricultural land only in 2005, seven years after I met Vasanti. Hers is not a land-owning family, but an analysis of her predicament would naturally lead us to notice that closely related inequity.

Thinking about such issues, we would be led to a study of the striking gender imbalance in India's population. Demographers estimate that where similar nutrition and health care are present, women live, on average, slightly longer than men—so we would expect a ratio of something like 102 women to 100 men. Instead, the most recent Indian census shows 92 women to 100 men. These numbers are averages. In the south, where property is transmitted through the maternal line, and where the husband moves into his bride's home rather than taking his bride away, women's basic life expectancy corresponds to the demographers' prediction: the state of Kerala has a sex ratio of 102 women to 100 men. In some northern states, by contrast, the ratio is alarmingly out of kilter: a house-to-house survey in one area of rural Bihar came up with the astounding figure of 75 women to 100 men. It's well known that these imbalances are augmented wherever information about the sex of the fetus is available. Amniocentesis clinics are ubiquitous throughout the nation. Because sex-selective abortion is such a widespread problem in India, it is illegal to seek information about the sex of the fetus, but these laws are rarely enforced.

Vasanti, then, has had a bit of good luck in being alive at all. Her family didn't nourish her very well, but they did better than many poor families. When I met her she seemed to be in reasonable health, and she is fortunate to have a strong constitution, since health care is not easily accessible to the poor in Gujarat. The Indian Constitution makes health a state rather than a federal issue, so there is great variation in the resources available to the poor state by state.

Some Indian states, for example, Kerala, have effective health care systems, but most do not.

Next, we are likely to notice the fact that a woman as intelligent and determined as Vasanti has had few employment options because she never learned to read and write. We can put this down to a failure in the Gujarati education system, since education, like health, is a state matter, and literacy rates vary greatly from state to state. In Kerala, adolescent literacy for both boys and girls is close to 100 percent, whereas nationally 75.3 percent of men are literate compared with only 53.7 percent of women. The factors that produce this discrepancy are related to those that produce the sex gap in basic life expectancy and health: women are thought to have fewer options in employment and politics, so from the family's perspective, it makes more sense to assign domestic labor to girls while sending boys to school. The prophecy is self-fulfilling, since illiteracy debars women from most employment and many political opportunities. Moreover, the fact that a girl will soon leave her birth family and join another family through marriage gives her parents a lesser stake in her future. Kerala has addressed these problems better than Gujarat, though Kerala has a poor record of creating employment opportunities for people once they are educated.

Because education is such a crucial avenue of opportunity, the Indian Constitution was amended in 2002 to give both primary and secondary education the status of an enforceable fundamental right. Recognizing that poor parents often keep children out of school because they need their labor to survive, the Supreme Court of India has ordered all schools to offer children a nutritious midday meal that contains at least 350 calories and 18 grams of protein, thus giving poor parents an economic incentive that often outweighs the lost wages from their child's labor during school hours.

Vasanti missed this change, which might have made her both literate and physically bigger.

Meanwhile, at the national level, the Constitution was amended
in 1992 to assign women one-third of the seats in local *panchayats,* or
village councils. This system, like the midday meal, provides incentives for parents to educate daughters as well as sons, since one day
they may well represent the interests of the family in local government. Again, this change came too late for Vasanti, in the sense that
it didn't influence her parents' educational choices for the family.
Now, however, Vasanti may utilize the adult education programs
offered by SEWA to enhance her participation in both politics and
employment.

Because Vasanti has had no formal education, she is cut off from
a full understanding of her nation's history and its political and
economic structure. (She can get news from TV and from her
friends, but she is still limited in her ability to access a more comprehensive account or to pursue issues that interest her.) She is also
unable to enjoy poetry, novels, or the many works of the imagination that would make her life richer and more fun. She is not, however, cut off from music and dance, and SEWA makes valuable use
of these media in educating women like Vasanti.

A key issue in Vasanti's story is domestic violence. That complex
story, in turn, involves social and governmental choices in many
areas. Her husband's alcoholism clearly fueled his violence. Several
Indian states have adopted prohibition laws for this very reason.
This hasn't proved to be a very effective remedy: more helpful would
have been educational programs about alcohol and drugs and high-
quality treatment and therapy, none of which were provided by state
government to Gujarat's poor population. By contrast, it was state
action rather than inaction that explains her husband's vasectomy:

bribing poor people to have vasectomies is not a great means of population control for many reasons, not the least of which is that it robs women of choice. As for the violence itself, Vasanti received no help from the police, a consequence of weak law enforcement and bad police training. So her bodily integrity and health were constantly at risk, and her dignity was violated.

When we think about domestic violence we have to think about exit options and bargaining power in the marriage. When a woman can leave, she doesn't have to endure being beaten. And when the husband knows she can leave because she has employment opportunities or control over property, she is at least somewhat less likely to be beaten. Important research by Bina Agarwal shows that landownership is the single most important factor explaining why some women in a region suffer domestic abuse and others don't. A woman who owns land is less likely to be victimized because she can leave the marriage, and when she leaves she will be taking something of great value with her. Other sources of leverage against an abusive husband are employment, education, movable property, and savings. A compassionate birth family also offers exit options. Vasanti's family was unusual in that they gave her the option to leave her husband with dignity, and even to take up employment. Nonetheless, the difficulty of getting a divorce—the legal system is slow and notoriously corrupt—made it hard for her to stand fully on her own.

The SEWA loan changed that picture. The organization gave Vasanti a source of support not tied to her status as a dependent; the money was hers to use even if she displeased her brothers. This independence enhanced her self-respect and capacity for choice.

The toll that domestic violence takes on physical health is enormous, but its effect on emotional health is equally devastating.

Women in Vasanti's position usually suffer greatly from both fear and the inhibition of anger. They often lack any true pleasure in love and sexual expression. The conditions that made it possible for Vasanti to leave her husband also improved her emotional health, as did her good relationship with her brothers. The SEWA loan opened still more doors to happiness: Vasanti clearly enjoys her friendship with Kokila and the experience of being respected and treated as an equal within a group of women.

During her marriage, Vasanti was cut off from all relationships except the highly unequal one with her abusive husband. She did not have friends, she was unable to work, she did not participate in politics. This is the lot of many women in abusive relationships, but it is particularly common for women whose caste status makes it shameful for them to seek employment outside the home. Upper-caste women like Vasanti are often worse off than lower-caste women, who can circulate freely. Vasanti was even prevented from having children, which would have provided her with a source of love. SEWA made it possible for her to become active in politics and to form a whole group of friends who respect her as an equal. The fact that she came to the SEWA office to tell her story to a stranger was itself a sign of new openness and curiosity. She seemed excited and proud to talk about her life. Nonetheless, the workplace options open to her as a Brahmin woman remain highly circumscribed, and her participation in political life is still limited by her inability to read and write.

Vasanti is active in one area of politics, as she and Kokila work to diminish domestic violence. We might ask, though, whether she knows her rights as a citizen, whether she is a voter, whether she knows anything about how to use the legal system. The *panchayat* system has done a great deal to enhance women's political engagement and knowledge, and India's poor in general have an extremely high level of participation in elections, so she probably has at least some understanding of the political system. In the absence of literacy and formal schooling, however, her ability to inform herself further is limited. Studies of the *panchayats* have shown that illiterate women have a hard time participating in public affairs and gaining respect.

SEWA focuses on a very basic theme that runs through all these issues: the ability of women to control and plan their own lives. SEWA teaches women that they are not merely passive, not objects to be pushed around by others or mere pawns or servants of others: they can make choices, they can plan their futures. This is a heady new idea for women brought up to think of themselves as dependents with no autonomy. In Vasanti's case, choice and independence were, indeed, the main difference between the SEWA loan and the loan from her brothers. The pleasure in this newfound status as a decision-maker seemed to pervade her relationship with Kokila (a chosen friend, and perhaps her first chosen friend) as well as her dealings with the women's group.

What else might we notice? We don't know much about Vasanti's working hours or the structure of her day. Does she have any time for leisure? Can she ever just sit and think, or enjoy something beautiful, or drink tea with her friends? She seems to take pleasure in dressing well. Her sari is a lovely color of bright blue; like most poor women in India, she does not allow poverty to restrict her aesthetic imagination. She can most likely enjoy play and leisure activity to some degree, not because her society has protected leisure time for all citizens, but because she has no children and no responsibilities for in-laws. The flip side of her sad story is that at least she is not stuck with the "double day" of a demanding job plus full responsibility for domestic labor and child and elder care, as are millions of women all over the world. In general, protecting leisure time for workers, especially female workers, is an important issue in creating a decent society.

In thinking about play and fun, I wondered if Vasanti was interested in meeting some nice men and perhaps marrying again, once her divorce was final. One of the most striking aspects of the Indian women's movement has been the virtual absence of Western romantic notions. Women who have endured an unhappy marriage rarely express interest in seeking another spouse. They want to be able to live without a man, and they love the fact that one of SEWA's central ideals is the Gandhian notion of self-sufficiency. The thought is that, just as India could not win self-respect and freedom without achieving self-sufficiency with regard to its colonial master, so women cannot have self-respect and freedom without extricating themselves from dependence on their colonial masters, namely, men. Women view their ability to live without a man as a sign of self-respect. We might wonder whether such women (who are often homophobic and thus unlikely to be involved in lesbian relationships) are deprived of one of life's great pleasures. Do they really choose to live as single women, or are they too emotionally traumatized or exhausted by malnutrition to seek out a partner? When they talk of Western notions of romance and express a preference for solidarity with a group of women, however, we are reminded that one way of life (in this case, as part of a romantic couple, whether opposite or same-sex) is not necessarily best for women everywhere.

Some of us, at least, might want to ask about Vasanti's relationship to the environment around her. Is it polluted? Is it dangerous? Does she have opportunities to think about environmental issues and to make choices for herself and others in that regard? Many women's movements are ecologically oriented; SEWA is not. Nor does the state in which Vasanti lives do much on such issues. Chances are, then, that Vasanti has no opportunity to be productively involved in environmental thinking, and her health may right now be at risk from environmental degradation (air pollution, poor water, and so on). Often women who lead the most allegedly "natural" lives are those most at risk, since cow dung, used for fuel in many poor countries, is one of the most damaging pollutants when it comes to respiratory health.

These are at least some of the aspects of Vasanti's situation that a concerned onlooker or reader, knowledgeable about her social context, would consider. Most of these issues are recognized as salient by SEWA and those close to Vasanti. Many were important to Vasanti all along. As she learns more about her situation and what produces it, other issues of which she might not have been aware (for example, the role of the *panchayat* system, or children's need for an adequate amount of protein) become important for her as well.

The diverse aspects of Vasanti's situation interact with one another in complex ways, as we can already see, but each one is also a distinct issue that must be addressed in its own right if Vasanti is to live the life she deserves. A decent public policy can influence all aspects of her experience. It makes sense for an approach to "development," which means making things better, to focus on how Vasanti's opportunities and freedoms to choose and act are affected by the variety of policies available for consideration.

Unfortunately, the dominant theoretical approaches in development economics, approaches used all over the world, are not allies of Vasanti's struggle. They do not "read" her situation the way a local activist or a concerned observer might. Nor, indeed, do they read it in a way that would make sense to Vasanti, or even in a way that respects her as a dignified human being with entitlements equal to those of others. They equate doing well (for a state or a nation) with an increase in GDP per capita. In other words, Gujarat is pursuing the right policies if and only if its economy is growing, and it should be compared with other Indian states simply by looking at GDP per capita.

What does that figure, however glorious, mean to Vasanti? It doesn't reach her life, and it doesn't solve her problems. Somewhere in Gujarat is increased wealth deriving from foreign investment, but she doesn't have it. To her, hearing that GDP per capita has increased nicely is like being told that somewhere in Gujarat there is a beautiful painting, only she can't look at it, or a table set with delicious food, only she can't have any. Increased wealth is a good thing in that it might have allowed the government to adopt policies that would have made a difference to Vasanti. That, however, has not happened, and we should not be surprised. In general, the benefits of increased wealth resulting from foreign investment go in the first instance to elites, and this is not simply because GDP is an average figure, neglecting distribution: as the Sarkozy Commission report shows, profits from foreign investment frequently do not even raise average household income. The benefits of this increased wealth do not reach the poor, unless those local elites are committed to policies of redistribution of wealth; and they particularly do not reach poor women, whose employment opportunities are so much worse than those of men. Nor, as research shows, does economic growth by itself deliver improvements in health and education, in the absence of direct state action. So the things that matter to Vasanti don't figure in the standard approach, whose single focus makes no difference to her life.

The standard approach, then, does not direct our attention to the reasons for Vasanti's inability to enjoy the fruits of her region's general prosperity. Indeed, it positively distracts attention from her problems by suggesting that the right way to improve the quality of life in Gujarat is to shoot for economic growth, and that alone.

In *Hard Times,* Charles Dickens portrayed a classroom in which children were taught the standard approach. Circus girl Sissy Jupe—who has only recently joined the class—is told to imagine that the classroom is a nation, and in that nation there are "fifty millions of money." Now, says the teacher, "Girl number twenty" (in keeping with the emphasis on aggregation, students have numbers rather than names), "isn't this a prosperous nation, and a'n't you in a thriving state?" Sissy bursts into tears and runs out of the room. She tells her friend Louisa that she could not answer the question, "unless I knew who had got the money and whether any of it was mine. But that had nothing to do with it. It was not in the figures at all."

What we seem to need is an approach that asks Sissy Jupe's question, an approach that defines achievement in terms of the opportunities open to each person. Such an approach had better begin close to the ground, looking at life stories and the human meaning of policy changes for real people. Developing policies that are truly pertinent to a wide range of human situations means attending to diverse factors that affect the quality of a human life—asking, in each area, "What are people (and what is each person) actually able to do and to be?" Of course any approach to development must employ devices of aggregation, but if aggregation is to deliver pertinent information, we must begin by asking carefully which items ought to be given prominence.

The elements of Vasanti's story have a very close relationship to the list of Central Capabilities that will be presented shortly. So it may seem that the way I tell Vasanti's story is circular, and that I single out those features only because I already know what's on the list. However, we can't look at a life or listen to a story without having some preliminary hunches about what is significant. That's the paradox of inquiry mentioned in Plato's *Meno:* if you don't have any idea what you're looking for, you won't ever find it. The paradox, however, need not prove disabling. What is important is that the search be not rigid but open to new learning. I have tried to learn a lot before framing the list, and stories like Vasanti's were key aspects of that learning experience (though not part of my justification of the list, as will be seen later). Nor is the list final: if it turns out to lack something that experience shows to be a crucial element of a life worthy of human dignity, it can always be contested and remade. Working with many activists over the years, and noticing what their experienced eyes notice as significant in the lives of women in their own societies, I have tried to educate my judgment accordingly, and continue to do so.

More recently, empirical work by Jonathan Wolff and Avner De-Shalit has confirmed that the capabilities on my list are the ones recognized as most salient in the immigrant communities in which they work (in Israel and Great Britain). Storytelling is never neutral; the narrator always directs attention to some features of the world rather than to others. We should, however, insist on genuine curiosity and theoretical flexibility in the construction of an alternative approach. The Capabilities Approach set out to be an alternative to the GDP approach that would incorporate these important virtues.

The Capabilities Approach has typically been elaborated in the context of international development policy, with a focus on poorer nations that are struggling to improve their quality of life. More recently, richer nations have compiled their own Human Development Reports, and their data have always been important in the Reports of the UN Human Development Reports Office. Still, the approach is sometimes thought of as suited only to poorer countries. All nations, however, contain struggles for lives worthy of human dignity, and all contain struggles for equality and justice. Vasanti's story has some features that would be found less often in the United States because it has a higher rate of literacy than does India. Inner-city schools in this country, however, often fail to deliver even functional literacy to their students, and at higher levels of education alarming inequalities in access remain. The experience of domestic violence is probably as common in the United States as it is in India, studies show, and strategies to combat it are still insufficient, despite increased public awareness of the problem and efforts by legal activists. Inequalities in health care and nutrition are ubiquitous in the United States, and this failure is unconscionable, given our nation's great wealth. All nations, then, are developing nations, in that they contain problems of human development and struggles for a fully adequate quality of life and for minimal justice. All are currently failing at the aim of ensuring dignity and opportunity for each person. For all, then, the Capabilities Approach supplies insight.

2

THE CENTRAL CAPABILITIES

The approach we are investigating is sometimes called the *Human Development Approach* and sometimes the *Capability* or *Capabilities Approach*. Occasionally the terms are combined, as in *Journal of Human Development and Capabilities*, the current name of the former *Journal of Human Development*—a title reflecting its new status as the official journal of the HDCA. To some extent these titles are used as mere verbal variants, and many people make no distinction among them. Insofar as there are any significant differences, "Human Development Approach" is associated, historically, with the Human Development Report Office of the United Nations Development Programme and its annual Human Development Reports. These reports use the notion of capabilities as a comparative measure rather than as a basis for normative political theory. Amartya Sen had a major intellectual role in framing them, but they do not incorporate all aspects of his (pragmatic and result-oriented) theory; they simply aim to package comparative information in such a way as to reorient the development and policy debate, rather than to advance a systematic economic or political theory.

"Capability Approach" and "Capabilities Approach" are the key terms in the political/economic program Sen proposes in works such as *Inequality Reexamined* and *Development as Freedom,* where the project is to commend the capability framework as the best space within which to make comparisons of life quality, and to show why it is superior to utilitarian and quasi-Rawlsian approaches. I typically use the plural, "Capabilities," in order to emphasize that the most important elements of people's quality of life are plural and qualitatively distinct: health, bodily integrity, education, and other aspects of individual lives cannot be reduced to a single metric without distortion. Sen, too, emphasizes this idea of plurality and nonreducibility, which is a key element of the approach.

I prefer the term "Capabilities Approach," at least in many contexts, to the term "Human Development Approach," because I am concerned with the capabilities of nonhuman animals as well as human beings. The approach provides a fine basis for a theory of justice and entitlement for both nonhuman animals and humans. Sen shares this interest, although he has not made it a central focus of his work.

The Capabilities Approach can be provisionally defined as an approach to comparative quality-of-life assessment and to theorizing about basic social justice. It holds that the key question to ask, when comparing societies and assessing them for their basic decency or justice, is, "What is each person able to do and to be?" In other words, the approach takes *each person as an end,* asking not just about the total or average well-being but about the opportunities available to each person. It is *focused on choice or freedom,* holding that the crucial good societies should be promoting for their people is a set of opportunities, or substantial freedoms, which people then may or may not exercise in action: the choice is theirs. It thus commits itself to respect for people's powers of self-definition. The approach is resolutely *pluralist about value:* it holds that the capability achievements that are central for people are different in quality, not just in quantity; that they cannot without distortion be reduced to a single numerical scale; and that a fundamental part of understanding and producing them is understanding the specific nature of each. Finally, the approach is *concerned with entrenched social injustice and inequality,* especially capability failures that are the result of discrimination or marginalization. It ascribes an urgent *task to government and public policy*—namely, to improve the quality of life for all people, as defined by their capabilities.

These are the essential elements of the approach. It has (at least) two versions, in part because it has been used for two different purposes. My own version, which puts the approach to work in constructing a theory of basic social justice, adds other notions in the process (those of *human dignity,* the *threshold, political liberalism*). As a theory of fundamental political entitlements, my version of the approach also employs a specific list of the *Central Capabilities.* Compared with many familiar theories of welfare, my approach also subtracts: my capability-based theory of justice refrains from offering a comprehensive assessment of the quality of life in a society, even for comparative purposes, because the role of *political liberalism* in my theory requires me to prescind from offering any comprehensive account of value. Sen's primary concern has been to identify capability as the most pertinent space of comparison for purposes of quality-of-life assessment, thus changing the direction of the development debate. His version of the approach does not propose a definite account of basic justice, although it is a normative theory and does have a clear concern with issues of justice (focusing, for example, on instances of capability failure that result from gender or racial discrimination). In consequence, Sen does not employ a threshold or a specific list of capabilities, although it is clear that he thinks some capabilities (for example, health and education) have a particular centrality. Nor does he make central theoretical use of the concept of *human dignity*, though he certainly acknowledges its importance. At the same time, Sen does propose that the idea of capabilities can be the basis for a comprehensive quality-of-life assessment in a nation, in that sense departing from the deliberately limited aims of my political liberalism.

These differences will occupy us further in Chapter 4. At this point, however, we may continue to treat the approach as a single, relatively unified approach to a set of questions about both quality of life and basic justice. The story of Vasanti and what is salient in her situation could have been told by either Sen or me, and the same essential features would have been recognized—although Sen would not formalize them as a list or make assessments of minimal social justice, choosing instead to focus on quality-of-life issues. Enough has been said, I hope, to draw attention to the shared contours of the approach and its guiding concepts, as well as to some specific concepts of my own version that will also be defined in this chapter, even though they do not figure centrally in Sen's theory.

What are *capabilities?* They are the answers to the question, "What is this person able to do and to be?" In other words, they are what Sen calls "substantial freedoms," a set of (usually interrelated) opportunities to choose and to act. In one standard formulation by Sen, "a person's 'capability' refers to the alternative combinations of functionings that are feasible for her to achieve. Capability is thus a kind of freedom: the substantive freedom to achieve alternative functioning combinations." In other words, they are not just abilities residing inside a person but also the freedoms or opportunities created by a combination of personal abilities and the political, social, and economic environment. To make the complexity of capabilities clear, I refer to these "substantial freedoms" as *combined capabilities*. Vasanti's combined capabilities are the totality of the opportunities she has for choice and action in her specific political, social, and economic situation.

Of course the characteristics of a person (personality traits, intellectual and emotional capacities, states of bodily fitness and health, internalized learning, skills of perception and movement) are highly relevant to his or her "combined capabilities," but it is useful to distinguish them from combined capabilities, of which they are but a part. I call these states of the person (not fixed, but fluid and dynamic) *internal capabilities*. They are to be distinguished from innate equipment: they are trained or developed traits and abilities, developed, in most cases, in interaction with the social, economic, familial, and political environment. They include such traits as Vasanti's learned political skill, or her skill in sewing; her newfound self-confidence and her freedom from her earlier fear. One job of a society that wants to promote the most important human capabilities is to support the development of internal capabilities—through education, resources to enhance physical and emotional health, support for family care and love, a system of education, and much more.

Why is it important to distinguish internal capabilities from combined capabilities? The distinction corresponds to two overlapping but distinct tasks of the decent society. A society might do quite well at producing internal capabilities but might cut off the avenues through which people actually have the opportunity to function in accordance with those capabilities. Many societies educate people so that they are capable of free speech on political matters—internally—but then deny them free expression in practice through repression of speech. Many people who are internally free to exercise a religion do not have the opportunity to do so in the sense of combined capability, because religious free exercise is not protected by the government. Many people who are internally capable of participating in politics are not able to choose to do so in the sense of combined capability: they may be immigrants without legal rights, or they may be excluded from participation in some other manner. It is also possible for a person to live in a political and social environment in which she could realize an internal capability (for example, criticizing the government) but lack the developed ability to think critically or speak publicly.

Because combined capabilities are defined as internal capabilities plus the social/political/economic conditions in which functioning can actually be chosen, it is not possible conceptually to think of a society producing combined capabilities without producing internal capabilities. We could, however, imagine a society that does well in creating contexts for choice in many areas but does not educate its citizens or nourish the development of their powers of mind. Some states in India are like this: open to those who want to participate but terrible at delivering the basic health care and education that would enable them to do so. Here, terminologically, we would say that neither internal nor combined capabilities were present, but that the society had done at least some things right. (And of course in such a society many people do have combined capabilities, just not the poor or the marginalized.) Vasanti's Gujarat has a high rate of political participation, like all Indian states: so it has done well in extending political capabilities to all. (Notice that here we infer the presence of the capability from the actual functioning: it seems hard to do otherwise empirically, but conceptually we ought to remember that a person might be fully capable of voting and yet choose not to vote.) Gujarat has not done similarly well in promoting related internal capabilities, such as education, adequate information, and confidence, for the poor, women, and religious minorities.

The distinction between internal and combined capabilities is not sharp, since one typically acquires an internal capability by some kind of functioning, and one may lose it in the absence of the opportunity to function. But the distinction is a useful heuristic in diagnosing the achievements and shortcomings of a society.

Internal capabilities are not innate equipment. The idea of innate equipment does, however, play a role in the Human Development Approach. After all, the term "human development" suggests the unfolding of powers that human beings bring into the world. Historically, the approach is influenced by philosophical views that focus on human flourishing or self-realization, from Aristotle to John Stuart Mill in the West and Rabindranath Tagore in India. And the approach in many ways uses the intuitive idea of waste and starvation to indicate what is wrong with a society that thwarts the development of capabilities. Adam Smith wrote that deprivation of education made people "mutilated and deformed in a[n] . . . essential part of the character of human nature." This captures an important intuitive idea behind the capabilities project. We therefore need a way to talk about these innate powers that are either nurtured or not nurtured, and for that we may use the term *basic capabilities*. We now know that the development of basic capabilities is not hardwired in the DNA: maternal nutrition and prenatal experience play a role in their unfolding and shaping. In that sense, even after a child is born we are always dealing with very early internal capabilities, already environmentally conditioned, not with a pure potential. Nonetheless, the category is a useful one, so long as we do not misunderstand it. Basic capabilities are the innate faculties of the person that make later development and training possible.

The concept of basic capabilities must be used with much caution, since we can easily imagine a theory that would hold that people's political and social entitlements should be proportional to their innate intelligence or skill. This approach makes no such claim. Indeed, it insists that the political goal for all human beings in a nation ought to be the same: all should get above a certain threshold level of combined capability, in the sense not of coerced functioning but of substantial freedom to choose and act. That is what it means to treat all people with equal respect. So the attitude toward people's basic capabilities is not a meritocratic one—more innately skilled people get better treatment—but, if anything, the opposite: those who need more help to get above the threshold get more help. In the case of people with cognitive disabilities, the goal should be for them to have the same capabilities as "normal" people, even though some of those opportunities may have to be exercised through a surrogate, and the surrogate may in some cases supply part of the internal capability if the person is unable to develop sufficient choice capability on her own, for example, by voting on that person's behalf even if the person is unable to make a choice. The one limitation is that the person has to be a child of human parents and capable of at least some sort of active striving: thus a person in a permanent vegetative condition or an anencephalic person would not be qualified for equal political entitlements under this theory. But the notion of basic capability is still appropriate in thinking about education: if a child has innate cognitive disabilities, special interventions are justified.

On the other side of capability is *functioning*. A functioning is an active realization of one or more capabilities. Functionings need not be especially active or, to use the term of one critic, "muscular." Enjoying good health is a functioning, as is lying peacefully in the grass. Functionings are beings and doings that are the outgrowths or realizations of capabilities.

In contrasting capabilities with functionings, we should bear in mind that capability means opportunity to select. The notion of *freedom to choose* is thus built into the notion of capability. To use an example of Sen's, a person who is starving and a person who is fasting have the same type of functioning where nutrition is concerned, but they do not have the same capability, because the person who fasts is able not to fast, and the starving person has no choice.

In a sense, capabilities are important because of the way in which they may lead to functionings. If people never functioned at all, in any way, it would seem odd to say that the society was a good one because it had given them lots of capabilities. The capabilities would be pointless and idle if they were never used and people slept all through life. In that limited way, the notion of functioning gives the notion of capability its end-point. But capabilities have value in and of themselves, as spheres of freedom and choice. To promote capabilities is to promote areas of freedom, and this is not the same as making people function in a certain way. Thus the Capabilities Approach departs from a tradition in economics that measures the real value of a set of options by the best use that can be made of them. Options are freedoms, and freedom has intrinsic value.

Some political views deny this: they hold that the right thing for government to do is to make people lead healthy lives, do worthwhile activities, exercise religion, and so on. We deny this: we say that capabilities, not functionings, are the appropriate political goals, because room is thereby left for the exercise of human freedom. There is a huge moral difference between a policy that promotes health and one that promotes health capabilities—the latter, not the former, honors the person's lifestyle choices.

The preference for capabilities is connected to the issue of respect for a plurality of different religious and secular views of life, and thus to the idea of political liberalism (defined in Chapter 4).

Children, of course, are different; requiring certain sorts of functioning of them (as in compulsory education) is defensible as a necessary prelude to adult capability.

Some people who use the Capabilities Approach think that in a few specific areas government is entitled to promote functionings rather than just capabilities. Richard Arneson, for example, has defended paternalistic function-oriented policies in the area of health: government should use its power to make people take up healthy lifestyles. Sen and I do not agree with this position because of the high value we ascribe to choice. There is one exception: government, I hold, should not give people an option to be treated with respect and nonhumiliation. Suppose, for example, that the U.S. government gave every citizen a penny that they could then choose to pay back to "purchase" respectful treatment. But if the person chose to keep the penny, the government would humiliate them. This is unacceptable. Government must treat all people respectfully and should refuse to humiliate them. I make this exception because of the centrality of notions of dignity and respect in generating the entire capabilities list. Similarly, virtually all users of the approach would agree that slavery should be prohibited, even if favored by a majority, and even if by voluntary contract.

Another area of reasonable disagreement involves the right to do things that would appear to destroy some or all capabilities. Should people be permitted to sell their organs? To use hard drugs? To engage in a wide range of risky sports? Typically we make compromises in such areas, and these compromises do not always make sense: thus alcohol, an extremely destructive drug, remains legal while marijuana is for the most part illegal. We regulate most sports for safety, but we do not have an organized public debate about which areas of freedom it makes sense to remove for safety's sake. We can certainly agree that capability-destruction in children is a particularly grave matter and as such should be off-limits. In other cases, reasonable safety regulation seems plausible—unless debate reveals that the removal of an option (boxing without gloves, say) is really an infringement of freedom so grave as to make people's lives incompatible with human dignity. Usually situations are not so grave, and thus in many such cases the approach has little to say, allowing matters to be settled through the political process.

This issue will be further illuminated if we turn to a related and crucial question: Which capabilities are the most important? The approach makes this valuational question central rather than concealing it. This is one of its attractive features. Other approaches always take some sort of stand on questions of value, but often without explicitness or argument. Sen and I hold that it is crucial to face this question head on, and to address it with pertinent normative arguments.

Sen takes a stand on the valuational issue by emphasis, choice of examples, and implication, but he does not attempt anything like a systematic answer, an issue to which we will return in Chapter 4. It is reasonable for him not to attempt a systematic answer, insofar as he is using the idea of capabilities merely to frame comparisons. Insofar as he is using it to construct a theory of democracy and of justice, it is less clear that his avoidance of commitments on substance is wise. Any use of the idea of capabilities for the purposes of normative law and public policy must ultimately take a stand on substance, saying that some capabilities are important and others less important, some good, and some (even) bad.

Returning to the idea of basic capabilities will help us grasp this point. Human beings come into the world with the equipment for many "doings and beings" (to use a common phrase of Sen's), and we have to ask ourselves which ones are worth developing into mature capabilities. Adam Smith, thinking of children deprived of education, said that their human powers were "mutilated and deformed." Imagine, instead, a child whose capacity for cruelty and the humiliation of others is starved and thwarted by familial and social development. We would not describe such a child as "mutilated and deformed," even if we granted that these capacities have their basis in innate human nature. Again, suppose we were told that a particular child was never taught to be capable of whistling *Yankee Doodle Dandy* while standing on her head. We would not say that this child's human powers had been "mutilated and deformed" because, even though the capability in question is not—unlike the capacity for cruelty—bad, and even though it is probably grounded in human nature, it is just not very important.

The Capabilities Approach is not a theory of what human nature is, and it does not read norms off from innate human nature. Instead, it is evaluative and ethical from the start: it asks, among the many things that human beings might develop the capacity to do, which ones are the really valuable ones, which are the ones that a minimally just society will endeavor to nurture and support? An account of human nature tells us what resources and possibilities we have and what our difficulties may be. It does not tell us what to value.

Nonhuman animals are less malleable than human animals, and

they may not be able to learn to inhibit a harmful capacity without painful frustration. They are also hard to "read," since their lives are not ours. Observing their actual capacities and having a good descriptive theory of each species and its form of life will thus rightly play a larger role in creating a normative theory of animal capabilities than it does in the human case. Still, the normative exercise is crucial, difficult though it may be.

How would we begin selecting the capabilities on which we want to focus? Much depends on our purpose. On the one hand, if our intention is simply comparative, all sorts of capabilities suggest interesting comparisons across nations and regions, and there is no reason to prescribe in advance: new problems may suggest new comparisons. On the other hand, if our aim is to establish political principles that can provide the grounding for constitutional law and public policy in a nation aspiring to social justice (or to propose goals for the community of nations), selection is of the utmost importance. We cannot select, however, using only the notion of capabilities. The title "Capabilities Approach" should not be read as suggesting that the approach uses only a single concept and tries to squeeze everything out of it.

At this point I invoke the notion of human dignity and of a life worthy of it—or, when we are considering other animal species, the dignity appropriate to the species in question. Dignity is an intuitive notion that is by no means utterly clear. If it is used in isolation, as if it is completely self-evident, it can be used capriciously and inconsistently. Thus it would be mistaken to use it as if it were an intuitively self-evident and solid foundation for a theory that would then be built upon it. My approach does not do this: dignity is one element of the theory, but all of its notions are seen as interconnected, deriving illumination and clarity from one another. (This

29

idea of a holistic and nonfoundational type of justification will be elaborated in Chapter 4.) In the case of dignity, the notion of respect is a particularly important relative, and the political principles themselves illuminate what we take human dignity (and its absence) to mean. But the basic idea is that some living conditions deliver to people a life that is worthy of the human dignity that they possess, and others do not. In the latter circumstance, they retain dignity, but it is like a promissory note whose claims have not been met. As Martin Luther King, Jr., said of the promises inherent in national ideals: dignity can be like "a check that has come back marked 'insufficient funds.'"

Although dignity is a vague idea that needs to be given content by placing it in a network of related notions, it does make a difference. A focus on dignity is quite different, for example, from a focus on satisfaction. Think about debates concerning education for people with severe cognitive disabilities. It certainly seems possible that satisfaction, for many such people, could be produced without educational development. The court cases that opened the public schools to such people used, at crucial junctures, the notion of dignity: we do not treat a child with Down syndrome in a manner commensurate with that child's dignity if we fail to develop the child's powers of mind through suitable education. In a wide range of areas, moreover, a focus on dignity will dictate policy choices that protect and support agency, rather than choices that infantilize people and treat them as passive recipients of benefit.

The claims of human dignity can be denied in many ways, but we may reduce them all to two, corresponding to the notions of internal capability and combined capability. Social, political, familial, and economic conditions may prevent people from choosing to function in accordance with a developed internal capability: this sort of thwarting is comparable to imprisonment. Bad conditions can, however, cut deeper, stunting the development of internal capabilities or warping their development. In both cases, basic human dignity remains: the person is still worthy of equal respect. In the former case, however, dignity has been more deeply violated. Think of the difference between rape and simple robbery. Both damage a person; neither removes the person's equal human dignity. Rape, however, can be said to violate a woman's dignity because it invades her internal life of thought and emotion, changing her relationship to herself.

The notion of dignity is closely related to the idea of active striving. It is thus a close relative of the notion of basic capability, something inherent in the person that exerts a claim that it should be developed. But whereas there is room to argue about whether innate potential differs across people, human dignity, from the start, is equal in all who are agents in the first place (again, excluding those in a permanent vegetative state and those who are anencephalic, thus without agency of any kind). All, that is, deserve equal respect from laws and institutions. If people are considered as citizens, the claims of all citizens are equal. Equality holds a primitive place in the theory at this point, although its role will be confirmed by its fit with the rest of the theory. From the assumption of equal dignity, it does not follow that all the centrally important capabilities are to be equalized. Treating people as equals may not entail equalizing the living conditions of all. The question of what treating people as equals requires must be faced at a later stage, with independent arguments.

In general, then, the Capabilities Approach, in my version, focuses on the protection of areas of freedom so central that their removal makes a life not worthy of human dignity. When a freedom is not that central, it will be left to the ordinary workings of the political process. Sometimes it is clear that a given capability is central in this way: the world has come to a consensus, for example, on the importance of primary and secondary education. It seems equally clear that the ability to whistle *Yankee Doodle Dandy* while standing on one's head is not of central importance and does not deserve a special level of protection. Many cases may be unclear for a long time: for example, it was not understood for many centuries that a woman's right to refuse her husband intercourse was a crucial right of bodily integrity. What must happen here is that the debate must take place, and each must make arguments attempting to show that a given liberty is implicated in the idea of human dignity. This cannot be done by vague intuitive appeals to the idea of dignity all by itself: it must be done by discussing the relationship of the putative entitlement to other existing entitlements, in a long and detailed process—showing, for example, the relationship of bodily integrity inside the home to women's full equality as citizens and workers, to their emotional and bodily health, and so forth. But there will be many unclear cases. What about the right to plural marriages? The right to homeschooling? Because the approach does not derive value from people's existing preferences (which may be distorted in various ways), the quality of the argument, not the number of supporters, is crucial. But it is evident that the approach will leave many matters as optional, to be settled by the political process.

Considering the various areas of human life in which people move and act, this approach to social justice asks, What does a life worthy of human dignity require? At a bare minimum, an ample threshold level of ten Central Capabilities is required. Given a widely shared understanding of the task of government (namely, that government has the job of making people able to pursue a dignified and minimally flourishing life), it follows that a decent political order must secure to all citizens at least a threshold level of these ten Central Capabilities:

1. *Life.* Being able to live to the end of a human life of normal length; not dying prematurely, or before one's life is so reduced as to be not worth living.

2. *Bodily health.* Being able to have good health, including reproductive health; to be adequately nourished; to have adequate shelter.

3. *Bodily integrity.* Being able to move freely from place to place; to be secure against violent assault, including sexual assault and domestic violence; having opportunities for sexual satisfaction and for choice in matters of reproduction.

4. *Senses, imagination, and thought.* Being able to use the senses, to imagine, think, and reason—and to do these things in a "truly human" way, a way informed and cultivated by an adequate education, including, but by no means limited to, literacy and basic mathematical and scientific training. Being able to use imagination and thought in connection with experiencing and producing works and events of one's own choice, religious, literary, musical, and so forth. Being able to use one's mind in ways protected by guarantees of freedom of expression with respect to both political and artistic speech, and freedom of religious exercise. Being able to have pleasurable experiences and to avoid nonbeneficial pain.

5. *Emotions.* Being able to have attachments to things and people outside ourselves; to love those who love and care for us, to grieve at their absence; in general, to love, to grieve, to experience longing, gratitude, and justified anger. Not having one's emotional develop-

ment blighted by fear and anxiety. (Supporting this capability means supporting forms of human association that can be shown to be crucial in their development.)

6. *Practical reason.* Being able to form a conception of the good and to engage in critical reflection about the planning of one's life. (This entails protection for the liberty of conscience and religious observance.)

7. *Affiliation.* (A) Being able to live with and toward others, to recognize and show concern for other human beings, to engage in various forms of social interaction; to be able to imagine the situation of another. (Protecting this capability means protecting institutions that constitute and nourish such forms of affiliation, and also protecting the freedom of assembly and political speech.) *(B)* Having the social bases of self-respect and nonhumiliation; being able to be treated as a dignified being whose worth is equal to that of others. This entails provisions of nondiscrimination on the basis of race, sex, sexual orientation, ethnicity, caste, religion, national origin.

8. *Other species.* Being able to live with concern for and in relation to animals, plants, and the world of nature.

9. *Play.* Being able to laugh, to play, to enjoy recreational activities.

10. *Control over one's environment.* (A) *Political.* Being able to participate effectively in political choices that govern one's life; having the right of political participation, protections of free speech and association. *(B) Material.* Being able to hold property (both land and movable goods), and having property rights on an equal basis with others; having the right to seek employment on an equal basis with others; having the freedom from unwarranted search and seizure. In work, being able to work as a human being, exercising practical reason and entering into meaningful relationships of mutual recognition with other workers.

Although this list pertains to human life, its general headings provide a reasonable basis for beginning to think more adequately about what we owe to nonhuman animals, a topic to be pursued in the final chapter.

Capabilities belong first and foremost to individual persons, and only derivatively to groups. The approach espouses a principle of *each person as an end.* It stipulates that the goal is to produce capabilities for each and every person, and not to use some people as a means to the capabilities of others or of the whole. This focus on the person makes a huge difference for policy, since many nations have thought of the family, for example, as a homogeneous unit to be supported by policy, rather than examining and promoting the separate capabilities of each of its members. At times group-based policies (for example, affirmative action) may be effective instruments in the creation of individual capabilities, but that is the only way they can be justified. This normative focus on the individual cannot be dislodged by pointing to the obvious fact that people at times identify themselves with larger collectivities, such as the ethnic group, the state, or the nation, and take pride in the achievements of that group. Many poor residents of Gujarat identify with that state's overall development achievements, even though they themselves don't gain much from them. The approach, however, considers each person worthy of equal respect and regard, even if people don't always take that view about themselves. The approach is not based on the satisfaction of existing preferences.

The irreducible heterogeneity of the Central Capabilities is extremely important. A nation cannot satisfy the need for one capability by giving people a large amount of another, or even by giving them some money. All are distinctive, and all need to be secured and protected in distinctive ways. If we consider a constitution that protects capabilities as essential rights of all citizens, we can see how this works in practice: people have a claim against government if their constitution protects religious freedom and that freedom has been violated—even though they may be comfortable, well-fed, and secure with respect to every other capability that matters.

The basic claim of my account of social justice is this: respect for human dignity requires that citizens be placed above an ample (specified) threshold of capability, in all ten of those areas. (By mentioning citizens, I do not wish to deny that resident aliens, legal and illegal, have a variety of entitlements: I simply begin with the core case.)

The list is a proposal: it may be contested by arguing that one or more of the items is not so central and thus should be left to the ordinary political process rather than being given special protection. Let's suppose someone asks why play and leisure time should be given that sort of protection. I would begin by pointing out that for many women all over the world, "the double day"—working at a job and then coming home to do all the domestic labor, including child care and elder care, is a crushing burden, impeding access to many of the other capabilities on the list: employment opportunities, political participation, physical and emotional health, friendships of many kinds. What play and the free expansion of the imaginative capacities contribute to a human life is not merely instrumental but partly constitutive of a worthwhile human life. That's the sort of case that needs to be made to put something on the list.

Sometimes social conditions make it seem impossible to deliver a threshold amount of all ten capabilities to everyone: two or more of them may be in competition. For example, poor parents in Vasanti's state may feel that they need to keep their children out of school in order to survive at all, since they need the wages from the child's labor to eke out an existence. In such a case, the economist's natural question is, "How do we make trade-offs?" However, when capabilities have intrinsic value and importance (as do the ten on my list), the situation produced when two of them collide is tragic: any course we select involves doing wrong to someone.

This situation of *tragic choice* is not fully captured in standard cost-benefit analysis: the violation of an entitlement grounded in basic justice is not just a large cost; it is a cost of a distinctive sort, one that in a fully just society no person has to bear.

Sen has argued that such tragic situations show a defect in standard economic approaches, which typically demand a complete ordering over all states of affairs. In tragic cases, he insists, we cannot rank one alternative above the other, and thus any good ordering will remain incomplete. Here there is a nuance of difference between his critique and mine. I would hold that not all tragic situations involve an inability to rank one state of affairs as better than another. We should distinguish between the presence of a tragic dilemma— any choice involves wrongdoing—and the impossibility of a ranking. Sometimes one choice may be clearly better than another in a tragic situation, even though all available choices involve a violation of some sort. (For the tragic hero Eteocles, in Aeschylus' play *Seven against Thebes,* it was a horrible wrong to choose to kill his brother, even though the alternative, which involved the destruction of the entire city, was clearly worse.) Sen is probably right that the demand for a complete ordering is misguided, but he is mistaken if he holds that all tragic dilemmas are cases in which no overall ordering is possible.

When we see a tragic choice—assuming that the threshold level of each capability has been correctly set—we should think, "This is very bad. People are not being given a life worthy of their human dignity. How might we possibly work toward a future in which the claims of all the capabilities can be fulfilled?" If the whole list has been wisely crafted and the thresholds set at a reasonable level, there usually will be some answer to that question. To return to India, the dilemma faced by poor parents was resolved by the state of Kerala, which pioneered a program of flexible school hours and also offered a nutritious midday meal that more than offset children's lost wages. The program has virtually wiped out illiteracy in the state. Seeing that it was possible for a relatively poor state to solve the problem by ingenuity and effort, the Supreme Court of India has made the midday meal mandatory for all government schools in the nation.

Such tragic choices abound in richer countries as well. In the United States, for example, a poor single mother may frequently be forced to choose between high-quality care for her child and a decent living standard, since some welfare rules require her to accept full-time work even when no care of high quality is available to her. Many women in the United States are forced to forgo employment opportunities in order to care for children or elderly relations; policies of family and medical leave, together with public provision of child and elder care, might address such dilemmas. One tragic choice ubiquitous in the United States is that between leisure time and a decent living standard (together with related health care benefits). It is widely known that Americans work longer hours than people in most other wealthy nations, and it is understood that family relations suffer in consequence, but the full measure of this tragic situation has not yet been taken. The capabilities perspective helps us see what is amiss here.

In other words, when we note a tragic conflict, we do not simply wring our hands: we ask what the best intervention point is to create a future in which this sort of choice does not confront people. We must also consider how to move people closer to the capability threshold right away, even if we can't immediately get them above it: thus, for example, equalizing access to primary education for all when we are not yet in a position to give everyone access to secondary education.

The Central Capabilities support one another in many ways. Two, however, appear to play a distinctive *architectonic* role: they organize and pervade the others. These two are *affiliation* and *practical reason*. They pervade the others in the sense that when the others are present in a form commensurate with human dignity, they are woven into them. If people are well-nourished but not empowered to exercise practical reason and planning with regard to their health and nutrition, the situation is not fully commensurate with human dignity: they are being taken care of the way we take care of infants. Good policy in the area of each of the capabilities is policy that respects an individual's practical reason; this is just another way of alluding to the centrality of choice in the whole notion of capability as freedom. What is meant by saying that the capability of practical reason organizes all the others is more obvious: the opportunity to plan one's own life is an opportunity to choose and order the functionings corresponding to the various other capabilities.

As for affiliation, the point is similar: it pervades the other capabilities in the sense that when they are made available in a way that respects human dignity, affiliation is part of them—the person is respected as a social being. Making employment options available without considering workplace relationships would not be adequate; nor would forms of health care that neglect, for example, people's needs to protect zones of intimacy by provisions for personal privacy. Affiliation organizes the capabilities in that deliberation about public policy is a social matter in which relationships of many kinds (familial, friendly, group-based, political) all play a structuring role.

The capabilities on the list are rather abstract: who specifies them further? For the most part, the answer is given by each nation's system of constitutional law, or its basic principles if it lacks a written constitution. There is room for nations to elaborate capabilities differently to some extent, given their different traditions and histories. The world community poses unique problems of specification because there is no overarching government, accountable to the people as a whole, that would supply the specification.

Part of the conception of the capabilities list, as we have already seen, is the idea of a *threshold*. The approach, in my version, is a partial theory of social justice: it does not purport to solve all distributional problems; it just specifies a rather ample social minimum. Delivering these ten capabilities to all citizens is a necessary condition of social justice. Justice may well require more: for example, the approach as developed thus far does not make any commitment about how inequalities above the minimum ought to be handled. Many approaches to social justice hold that an ample threshold is not sufficient. Some demand strict equality; John Rawls insists that inequalities can be justified only where they raise the level of the worst-off. The Capabilities Approach does not claim to have answered these questions, although it might tackle them in the future.

The threshold does, however, require equality in some cases. It is a difficult question how far adequacy of capability requires equality of capability. Such a question can be answered only by detailed thought about each capability, by asking what respect for equal human dignity requires. I argue, for example, that respect for equal human dignity requires equal voting rights and equal rights to religious freedom, not simply an ample minimum. A system that allotted to women one-half of the votes it allots to men would be manifestly disrespectful, as would a system that gave members of minority religions some freedom but not the same degree of freedom as is given to the majority. (For example, if Christians could celebrate their holy day without penalty because work days are arranged that way, but Jews and Seventh Day Adventists would be fired for refusing to work on a Saturday, that system would raise manifest problems of justice.) All the political entitlements, I argue, are such that inequality of distribution is an insult to the dignity of the unequal. Similarly, if some children in a nation have educational opportunities manifestly unequal to those of other children, even though all get above a minimum, this seems to raise an issue of basic fairness—as Justice Thurgood Marshall famously argued in a case concerning the Texas public schools. Either equality or something near to it may be required for adequacy.

But the same may not be true of entitlements in the area of material conditions. Having decent, ample housing may be enough: it is not clear that human dignity requires that everyone have exactly the same type of housing. To hold that belief might be to fetishize possessions too much. The whole issue needs further investigation.

Setting the threshold precisely is a matter for each nation, and, within certain limits, it is reasonable for nations to do this differently, in keeping with their history and traditions. Some questions will remain very difficult: in such cases, the Capabilities Approach tells us what to consider salient, but it does not dictate a final assignment of weights and a sharp-edged decision. (The contours of an abortion right, for example, are not set by the approach, although it does tell us what to think about in debating this divisive issue.) Even at the level of threshold-drawing, the ordinary political process of a well-functioning democracy plays, rightly, an ineliminable role.

Another question raised by the idea of a threshold is that of utopianism. At one extreme, we might specify such a high threshold that no nation could meet it under current world conditions. Tragic conflicts would be ubiquitous, and even ingenuity and effort would not be able to resolve them. At the other end of the spectrum is lack of ambition: we might set the threshold so low that it is easy to meet, but less than what human dignity seems to require. The task for the constitution-maker (or, more often, for courts interpreting an abstract constitution and for legislators proposing statutes) is to select a level that is aspirational but not utopian, challenging the nation to be ingenious and to do better.

Many questions remain about how to do this: for example, should the threshold be the same in every nation, despite the fact that nations begin with very different economic resources? To say otherwise would seem to be disrespectful to people who by sheer chance are born in a poorer nation; to say yes, however, would require nations to meet some of their obligations at least partially through redistribution from richer to poorer nations. It might also be too dictatorial, denying nations a right to specify things somewhat differently, given their histories and situations.

The Capabilities Approach has recently been enriched by Jonathan Wolff and Avner De-Shalit's important book *Disadvantage*. In addition to providing support for the list of the ten Central Capabilities, and in addition to developing strong arguments in favor of recognizing irreducibly heterogeneous goods, Wolff and De-Shalit introduce some new concepts that enhance the theoretical apparatus of the Capabilities Approach. The first is that of *capability security*. They argue, plausibly, that public policy must not simply give people a capability, but give it to them in such a way that they can count on it for the future. Consider Vasanti: when she had a loan from her brothers, she had a range of health- and employment-related capabilities, but they were not secure, since her brothers could call in the loan at any point, or turn her out of the house. The SEWA loan gave her security: so long as she worked regularly, she could make the payments and even build up some savings.

Working with new immigrant groups in their respective countries (Britain and Israel), Wolff and De-Shalit find that security about the future is of overwhelming importance in these people's ability to use and enjoy all the capabilities on the list. (Notice that a feeling of security is one aspect of the capability of "emotional health," but they are speaking of both emotions and reasonable expectations—capability security is an objective matter and has not been satisfied if government bewitches people into believing they are secure when they are not.) The security perspective means that for each capability we must ask how far it has been protected from the whims of the market or from power politics. One way nations often promote capability security is through a written constitution that cannot be amended except by a laborious supramajoritarian process. But a constitution does not enforce itself, and a constitution contributes to security only in the presence of adequate access to the courts and justified confidence in the behavior of judges.

Thinking about capability security makes us want to think about political procedure and political structure: What form of political organization promotes security? How much power should courts have, and how should their role be organized? How should legislatures be organized, what voting procedures should they adopt, and

43

how can the power of interest groups and lobbies to disrupt the political process be constrained? What are the roles of administrative agencies and expert knowledge in promoting citizens' capabilities? We shall return to these issues—as yet underexplored in the Capabilities Approach—in the final chapter.

Wolff and De-Shalit introduce two further concepts of great interest: *fertile functioning* and *corrosive disadvantage*. A fertile functioning is one that tends to promote other related capabilities. (At this point they do not distinguish as clearly as they might between functioning and capability, and I fear that alliteration has superseded theoretical clarity.) They argue plausibly that affiliation is a fertile functioning, supporting capability-formation in many areas. (Do they really mean that it is the functioning associated with affiliation, or is it the capability to form affiliations that has the good effect? This is insufficiently clear in their analysis.) Fertile functionings are of many types, and which functionings (or capabilities) are fertile may vary from context to context. In Vasanti's story, we can see that access to credit is a fertile capability, for the loan enabled her to protect her bodily integrity (not returning to her abusive husband), to have employment options, to participate in politics, to have a sense of emotional well-being, to form valuable affiliations, and to enjoy enhanced self-respect. In other contexts, education plays a fertile role, opening up options of many kinds across the board. Landownership can sometimes have a fertile role, protecting a woman from domestic violence, giving her exit options, and generally enhancing her status. Corrosive disadvantage is the flip side of fertile capability: it is a deprivation that has particularly large effects in other areas of life. In Vasanti's story, subjection to domestic violence was a corrosive disadvantage: this absence of protection for her bodily integrity jeopardized her health, emotional well-being, affiliations, practical reasoning, and no doubt other capabilities as well.

The point of looking for fertile capabilities/functionings and corrosive disadvantages is to identify the best intervention points for public policy. Each capability has importance on its own, and all citizens should be raised above the threshold on all ten capabilities. Some capabilities, however, may justly take priority, and one reason to assign priority would be the fertility of the item in question, or its tendency to remove a corrosive disadvantage. This idea helps us think about tragic choices, for often the best way of preparing a tragedy-free future will be to select an especially fertile functioning and devote our scarce resources to that.

3

A NECESSARY COUNTER-THEORY

Development economics is not just an academic discipline; it has wide-ranging influence on our world. Reigning theories in the field influence the choices of political leaders and policymakers, whether directly, through their own appreciation of these theories, or indirectly, through advice they get from their economists and from international agencies such as the IMF and the World Bank. Although the dominant theories in development economics have an especially strong influence on poorer nations, which are particularly dependent on the policies of the World Bank and the IMF, these theories influence lives everywhere. Indeed, the ways of thinking that they embody are used whenever nations plan to improve their quality of life, or maintain that they have done so. A need to confront these dominant models has been felt internationally. In fact France, a very rich nation, launched the influential rethinking of quality-of-life measurement (heavily influenced by the Capabilities Approach) that became known as the Sarkozy Commission, and much of the data used in the commission's analysis comes from the richer nations. When we consider theories of development, then, we are considering what people in every nation are striving for: a decent quality of life.

The GDP Approach

For many years, the reigning model in development economics measured the progress of a country by looking at economic growth as measured by GDP per capita. This approach had its advantages: GDP is relatively easy to measure, since the monetary value of goods and services makes it possible to compare quantities of different types. Moreover, GDP has attractive transparency: it is difficult for countries to fudge the data to make themselves look better. And economic growth is at least a step in the right direction, so it seems reasonable to look at it as at least one indication of a nation or region's relative achievement. Many development practitioners, moreover, were strongly influenced by the so-called trickle-down theory, so common in the 1980s and 1990s, which suggested that the benefits of economic growth are bound to improve the lot of the poor, even if no direct action is taken in that direction.

That theory has now been shown to be questionable in a number of ways. For example, the comparative studies of Indian states carried out by Jean Drèze and Amartya Sen (a particularly good thing to study, since these states share a set of political institutions but have pursued utterly different policies in matters of growth as well as in health and education) have shown that increased economic growth does not automatically improve quality of life in important areas such as health and education. Other data, for example, the comparison between India and China over the past sixty years, show that increased GDP is not correlated with the emergence and stability of political liberty. India has done dramatically worse than China on GDP, and yet it is an extremely stable democracy, with well-protected fundamental liberties; China is not. Moreover, the data assembled in the Human Development Reports themselves show that national rankings generated by the Human Development Index (HDI), which factors in education and longevity, are not the same as those generated by average GDP alone: the United States, for example, slips from number 1 in GDP to number 12 in the HDI, and it is even lower on other specific capabilities. In the 1980s, however, these facts were not known, so the GDP theory seemed more plausible then than it ever could now as a way of measuring relative quality of life—even to people who really cared about the condition of the poor and about the quality of health care and education.

Development is a normative concept. It means, or should mean, that things are getting better. So to rank nations in accordance with their GDP per capita suggested that those at the top were doing better by their people, that human lives were going better. Sometimes that implication was made explicit: average GDP was taken to be a measure of the quality of life in a nation. The problems with that way of looking at nations and regions should by now be all too evident, but we can still spell them out.

First, even if we were committed to measuring quality of life in narrowly monetary terms, and committed, as well, to using a single average number rather than to looking at distribution, it is far from clear that GDP per capita is the most interesting notion to consider. As the report of the Sarkozy Commission suggests, average real household income seems more pertinent to people's actual living standard, and increase in GDP is not very well correlated with increase in average household income, particularly in a world of globalization, where profits may be repatriated by foreign investors without contributing to the spending power of a country's citizens. Moreover, as a gross rather than a net measure, GDP does not account for the depreciation of capital goods. At the very least, then, users of GDP should acknowledge that other national measures are also significant and that the household perspective, in particular, needs to be taken into account. Once we concede that point—as the Sarkozy Commission also argues—there are compelling reasons to go much further, by granting that the value of nonmarket household work must also be factored in, since domestic labor is a substitute for goods and services that would otherwise have to be purchased in the market. But this value is not captured, even in current measures of average household income. Even at the simplest economic level, GDP is increasingly contested, and no easy single replacement is on the horizon.

Second, the GDP approach, and all similar approaches based upon a national average, do not look at distribution and can give high marks to nations that contain enormous inequalities, suggesting that such nations are on the right track. South Africa under apartheid, with its immense inequalities, used to shoot to the top of the list of developing countries: it had plenty of assets, and if we divide the wealth by the number of people in the country, we get a good ratio, since the amount is so large. Obviously enough, that ratio doesn't tell us where the wealth is located, who controls it, and what happens to the people who don't.

The GDP approach fails not only to look at the life quality of the poor but also to ask a question that the South Africa example forcefully suggests: Are there groups within the population, racial, religious, ethnic, or gender groups, that are particularly marginalized and deprived?

Third, the GDP approach aggregates across component parts of lives, suggesting that a single number will tell us all we need to know about quality of life, when in reality it doesn't give us good information. It funnels together aspects of human life that are both distinct and poorly correlated with one another: health, longevity, education, bodily security, political rights and access, environmental quality, employment opportunities, leisure time, and still others. Even if all citizens of South Africa had the amount of wealth given in the GDP average figure, that number would not tell us how they are doing in these diverse areas. Countries of similar average GDP can differ radically in the quality of their health care systems, the quality of public education, their political rights and liberties. (Thus the GDP model has at times encouraged uncritical China-worship: things must be pretty good there, if economic growth is so robust.) Of course such differences are often augmented by the power discrepancies just mentioned: even if we assume that majorities and minorities have equal wealth and income (which they usually don't), they may have very unequal religious freedom, political access, or security from violence.

By failing to make salient the issue of distribution, the importance of political freedom, the possible subordination of minorities, and the separate aspects of lives that deserve attention, the GDP approach distracts attention from these urgent matters, suggesting that when a nation has improved its average GDP, it is "developing" well.

Even to the extent that GDP is a good proxy for other capabilities, it is at best only a proxy, and it does not tell us what's really important. Since the important things are open to study, it seems to make sense to go directly to them. Specifying ends itself has a policy effect, reminding us forcefully that real human importance is located not in GDP but elsewhere.

The Utilitarian Approach

One step up from GDP, in terms of adequacy, is another common economic approach that measures quality of life in a nation by looking at either total or average utility, where utility is understood as the satisfaction of preferences. (This approach has its roots in political philosophy, and its more philosophical version will be considered in Chapter 4.) The utilitarian approach has the merit of caring about people: it measures quality of life according to people's reported feelings about their lives. And it has the great merit that Jeremy Bentham, the founder of utilitarianism, claimed: "Each [is] to count for one, and none for more than one." That is, the satisfaction of person A counts for the same as the satisfaction of person B, even if A is a peasant and B is a king. Each gets one vote. So the theory is potentially quite democratic—even, in the context of established hierarchy, radical. That is exactly what Bentham intended. People who denigrate utilitarianism as cold-hearted or in league with big business often wrongly forget its radical origins and commitments.

Intentions are not everything, however. There are four problems with the utilitarian approach as a measure of quality of life in a nation that make it both less democratic than it seems and a misleading guide to public policy.

First, like the GDP approach, it aggregates across lives. Even though it looks at satisfactions rather than at wealth—and thus doesn't utterly ignore the poor person who might lack wealth altogether (as does the GDP approach)—it has a similar problem. A nation can get a very high average or total utility so long as a lot of people are doing quite well, even if a few people at the bottom of the social ladder are suffering greatly. Indeed, the approach justifies the infliction of a very miserable life on an underclass, so long as this strategy raises the average satisfaction level. Even slavery and torture are ruled out—insofar as they are—only by uncertain empirical arguments claiming that slavery and torture are inefficient.

Second, like the GDP approach again, the utilitarian approach aggregates across components of lives. The term "satisfaction," like "pleasure," the other term often used by utilitarians as an all-purpose metric, suggests singleness and commensurability, where real life suggests diversity and incommensurability. Think about the satisfaction we feel in eating a good meal. How can that be compared to the pleasure or satisfaction we get from helping a friend in need, or raising a child, or listening to a harrowing but profound piece of music? How might we even begin commensurating the pleasure of listening to Mahler's 10th Symphony with the pleasure of eating an ice-cream cone? The very idea seems ludicrous. We usually don't make such comparisons: we think that human life contains pleasures, or satisfactions, of many different kinds. If you were asked, "How satisfied are you with your life?"—the sort of question utilitarian social scientists are fond of asking—you would be strongly inclined to say something like, "Well, my health is great, my work is going well, but one of my friends is sick and I'm very worried about that." Utilitarian social scientists, however, do not permit that sort of normal complex human reply. They frame surveys so that there's just a single scale, and people have to choose a single number. The fact that so many individuals still answer the question does not show us that they agree with the question-asker's view that satisfactions are all commensurable on a single scale. If it shows us anything, it's something we already know: that people are deferential to authority. If a person in authority has framed the questionnaire a certain way, we just have to go along with it, even if it seems pretty crude. After all, those who don't answer because they object to the way the question is framed don't get counted in the result.

In short, the utilitarian approach seems to care about people, but it doesn't care about them all that deeply, and its commitment to a single metric effaces a great deal about how people seek and find value in their lives. Bentham was not willfully hard-hearted or crass, but he was a man with a limited imagination. As his pupil John Stuart Mill said in his great essay "Bentham," "In many of the most natural and strongest feelings of human nature he had no sympathy; from many of its graver experiences he was altogether cut off; and the faculty by which one mind understands a mind different from itself . . . was denied him by his deficiency of Imagination."

Bentham, Mill, and many modern utilitarian economists (for example, Gary Becker) equate utility with some real psychological state, such as pleasure or satisfaction, which can be identified independent of choice and is held to lie behind choice. Another form of utilitarianism conceives of preferences as revealed in choice. There are complex and technical arguments between these two positions in economics that cannot be reconstructed here. One of Sen's important achievements in economics, however, has been to show that there are insuperable difficulties with the revealed preference approach. In "Internal Consistency of Choice," he demonstrates that preferences so construed do not even obey basic axioms of rationality, such as transitivity. (If A is preferable to B, and B is preferable to C, transitivity says that A is preferable to C.) For this reason, I confine my critique to what I take to be the stronger version of preference utilitarianism.

It's possible to imagine the utilitarian approach responding to my first and second criticisms: to the first, by adopting a separate account of a social minimum; to the second, by admitting that utility has plural dimensions. John Stuart Mill made the second correction, proposing qualitative distinctions within utility. In his important article "Plural Utility," Sen follows Mill's lead. And Mill made at least a beginning of responding to the first point, by giving political rights a secure position, apparently outside the utilitarian calculus.

A third objection, however, cuts deeper, requiring us to depart from the utility-based standard altogether. This objection, made famous by Sen and Jon Elster, focuses on the social malleability of preferences and satisfactions. Preferences are not hard-wired: they respond to social conditions. When society has put some things out of reach for some people, they typically learn not to want those things; they form what Elster and Sen call *adaptive preferences*. Sometimes adaptation happens after the person wanted the thing initially: Elster's book *Sour Grapes* takes its title from the fable of the fox who starts calling the grapes sour after he finds that he can't reach them. Sometimes, however, people learn not to want the goods in the first place, because these goods are put off-limits for people of their gender, or race, or class. Women brought up on images of the proper woman as one who does not work outside the home, or who does not get very much schooling, often don't form a desire for such things, and thus they may report satisfaction with their state, even though opportunities that they would have enjoyed using are being denied them. Other marginalized groups also often internalize their second-class status. By defining the social goal in terms of the satisfaction of actual preferences, utilitarian approaches thus often reinforce the status quo, which may be very unjust.

Sen's work on adaptive preferences focuses on these lifelong adaptations. Sen shows that even at the level of physical health, people's expectations and reports of good or bad status reflect social expectations. Comparing health reports of widows and widowers in Bengal, he found that widowers were full of complaints: after all, they had lost the person who used to wait on them hand and foot. Widows, who were actually doing much worse by an independent medical assessment, had few complaints: after all, society told them that they had no right to continue to exist after their husband's death.

Vasanti's life brings such problems sharply to the fore, since she would never have reported dissatisfaction with illiteracy, or with being cut off from political participation, before the consciousness-raising experience in the SEWA group showed her the importance of these capabilities and encouraged her to think of herself as a person whose worth is equal to that of others. Although she certainly did not adapt to domestic violence, she did adjust to a life that lacked some of the Central Capabilities on the list—until she was led to see their value.

A fourth and final objection is also forceful: the utilitarian approach I have described focuses on satisfaction as a goal. Satisfaction is usually understood as a state or condition of the person that follows activity; it is not itself a form of activity, and it can even be achieved without the associated activity. For example, a person can feel satisfied about a job well done even though she has done nothing, but has been deluded into believing that she has. The philosopher Robert Nozick made this point vividly by imagining an "experience machine": hooked up to such a device, you would have the illusion that you were loving, working, or eating, and you would have the experiences of satisfaction associated with those activities— but in reality you would be doing nothing at all. Most people, bets Nozick, would not choose the experience machine. They would prefer a life of choice and activity, even knowing in advance that many of the activities would end in frustration. Most of his readers agree.

In short, the utilitarian approach undervalues freedom. Freedom can be valued as a means to satisfaction, and here there can be agreement between utilitarians and capability theorists, since we, too, emphasize the instrumental importance of freedom. Freedom to choose and to act, however, is an end as well as a means, and it is this aspect that the standard utilitarian position cannot capture.

In the context of lives like Vasanti's, the issue of choice and agency looms large. Women are often treated as passive dependents, creatures to be cared for (or not), rather than as independent human beings deserving respect for their choices. In other words, they are often infantilized. We think that within limits satisfaction is an appropriate goal for infants—although we want them to try to initiate activity quite soon, even if it brings them frustration. Certainly a passive state of satisfaction is not an appropriate goal for adult human beings. There's a great difference between a public policy that aims to take care of people and a public policy that aims to honor choice. Even in the area of nutrition, where we might initially think satisfaction is all we want, we can see that a policy that just doles out food to people rather than giving them choice in matters of nutrition is insufficiently respectful of their freedom. This is a version of the point we made when we said that practical reason pervades all the other goals, making their pursuit worthy of human dignity.

Resource-Based Approaches

A popular alternative to the utilitarian approach is a group of approaches that urges the equal (or more distributively adequate) allocation of basic resources, understanding wealth and income to be such all-purpose resources. Amartya Sen often criticizes such approaches, focusing on John Rawls's theory of the "primary goods" in *A Theory of Justice*. Given, however, that for Rawls the primary goods are just one element in a highly complex overall theory, it is perhaps best not to invoke his theory, but to consider a simpler proposal, namely, that a country does better the more resources it has, *so long as it divides them equally (or equally enough) among all citizens.* Let us call this the "resource-based approach." This approach is an egalitarian version of the GDP approach.

This program has the merit of caring greatly about distribution. However, it, too, encounters formidable objections. First of all, income and wealth are not good proxies for what people are actually able to do and to be. People have differing needs for resources if they are to attain a similar level of functioning, and they also have different abilities to convert resources into functionings. Some of the pertinent differences are physical: a child needs more protein than an adult for healthy physical functioning, and a pregnant or lactating woman needs more nutrients than a nonpregnant woman. A sensible public policy would not give equal nutrition-related resources to all, but would (for example) spend more on the protein needs of children, since the sensible policy goal is not just spreading some money around but giving people the ability to function. Money is just an instrument.

Some of the pertinent differences, moreover, are created by persistent social inequalities, and here the resource-based approach, like the approaches previously considered, proves an ally of the status quo. In order to put women and men in a similar position with respect to educational opportunity in a society that strongly devalues female education, we will have to spend more on female education than on male education. If we want people with physical disabilities to be able to move around in society as well as "normal" people, we will need to spend extra money on them, retrofitting buildings with ramps, buses with lifts, and so forth. The two cases are similar: the reason the extra expense is required is that society has proceeded unjustly in the past, building the social environment in ways that marginalize certain people. But even if we take a case in which the extra expenditure is not remedial, it may still be justified, though the argument is different: a child born with Down syndrome may prove more expensive to educate than other children, but a society committed to educating all its citizens should not shrink from that expense. The important point for our purposes is that in neither case does the resource-based approach tell us enough about how people are really doing. It could give high marks to a nation that ignores the protests of marginalized or subordinated groups.

Income and wealth are not adequate proxies for ability to function in many areas. They are especially bad proxies, perhaps, for social respect, inclusion, and nonhumiliation. Societies often contain groups that are reasonably wealthy but socially excluded: Jews in eighteenth- and nineteenth-century Europe, gays and lesbians in the twentieth-century United States. Even if we equalized wealth and income completely, we would not be rid of stigma and discrimination.

There are some goods, moreover, that might be completely or largely absent in a society in which wealth and income are both reasonably high and fairly equally distributed. Such a society might still lack religious freedom, or the freedom of speech and association. Or it might have these and yet lack access to a reasonably unpolluted environment. GDP per capita, even equally distributed, is not a good proxy for these other important goods. If we think that all these things are important, we want public policy to focus on each of them, rather than suggesting that they have all been achieved by a focus on income and wealth.

Capabilities and the Measurement Question

Out of these discontents was born the idea that the real question one must ask is, What are people actually able to do and to be? What real opportunities for activity and choice has society given them? The approach in all its forms—both the comparative theory of quality of life employed by Sen and by development economists under his influence, and the theory of minimal justice that I have developed—insists on the heterogeneity and incommensurability of all the important opportunities or capabilities, the salience of distribution, and the unreliability of preferences as indices of what is really worth pursuing.

Readers of the Human Development Reports of the United Nations Development Programme will notice that they still rank nations using a single metric, the Human Development Index. The HDI is a weighted aggregate of data concerning life expectancy, educational attainment, and GDP per capita. (The weightings are explained in a technical appendix to each of the reports.) We might object, then, that the HDI is guilty of the same oversimplifications of which the other approaches have been accused. This objection, however, misunderstands the role of the HDI. The HDI is strategic. It was inserted into the first report late in the process of formulation, over the objections of some purists, because Mahbub ul Haq, a consummate pragmatist, believed that nations accustomed to seeing a single ranking would accept nothing else, and the reports would have no impact unless they came up with some single ranking. What was important was to make it a different single number, one that heavily weighted items (longevity, education) not typically emphasized in development rankings. Then, having arrested people's attention by that different single number, dramatizing the importance of health and education, one could hope that people would go behind the first table and read the disaggregated data laid out in the rest of the report. The disaggregated data are where the action is, but a single number, seen as suggestive rather than final, can direct the mind to certain salient aspects of the data.

Over the years, the reports have kept the HDI and the disaggregated data, but they have also added other suggestive aggregations. The GDI (Gender Development Index) corrects the HDI for gender imbalance, and countries that prided themselves on their high ranking in the HDI (for example, Japan) were shocked to find themselves well down the list in the GDI. The GEM (Gender Empowerment Measure) measures not women's attainments in longevity and education but their access to managerial and political positions. This, too, has proven illuminating, since in many cases there is a significant discrepancy between the GDI and the GEM: thus the GEM, though an aggregate, directs the reader to ponder the separate importance of managerial and political power as elements in women's equality. Other suggestive aggregations have been added. Finally, each report has a theme (technology, human rights, and so on), and essays full of data are written around each theme. Nobody using the reports, then, could get the impression that a single number is all that matters. Single numbers lead the mind to pertinent Central Capabilities.

It is natural to wonder whether, and how, capabilities can be measured. People tend to succumb to what might be called "the fallacy of measurement"; that is, noting that a certain thing (let's say GDP) is easy to measure, they become convinced that this thing is the most pertinent or the most central thing. Of course that does not follow. But the proponent of a new standard of value for public action still needs to show that in principle we can find ways to measure that value. Capabilities are plural, but that does not mean that each of them cannot be measured singly. The difficulty is that the notion of capability combines internal preparedness with external opportunity in a complicated way, so that measurement is likely to be no easy task. This question rightly occupies many workers on the approach, and a large literature on the measurement of capabilities is developing. Sometimes we may have to infer capability from patterns of functioning. Suppose, for example, we observed that African-Americans have low voter turnout. We could not directly infer that this absence of functioning was also an absence of capability, since people might just choose not to vote. However, when a pattern of low functioning correlates with social subordination and stigma, we might suspect that some subtle impediments really are interfering with political capability. These might include barriers to voter registration, difficulty accessing polling places, and denigration of these voters at the polling place; they might also include educational inequality, persistent feelings of hopelessness, and other less tangible capability failures. But the complexity of the question does not mean that it is not real and susceptible of study: so the right response to the complexity is to work harder at identifying and measuring the pertinent factors. Similarly, when we want to know whether people have access to play and recreation, we would begin with the obvious, looking at working hours and leisure time. We would soon, however, be led into more complex issues, such as the location, maintenance, and safety of parks and other recreational facilities.

People often think of measurement as involving a numerical scale of some type. In real life, however, we are familiar with other, more qualitative styles of measurement. When the U.S. Supreme Court asks whether a given law violates the First Amendment's guarantee of freedom of speech, the Court does not use a numerical scale on which various speech regimes are lined up; instead, it consults the text of the Constitution, its own precedents, and other pertinent historical and social materials. Nonetheless, it seems correct to say that the Court has decided whether a given policy puts some citizens beneath an acceptable threshold where the freedom of speech is concerned. Some capabilities, I suggest, need to be measured in this way and not on a quantitative scale at all. If we thought that a numerical scale would have been helpful in cases involving the freedom of speech, or the freedom of religion, we would probably have used one. Instead, the discursive form of analysis that has evolved seems appropriate for at least some questions involving a threshold level of a fundamental entitlement.

Human Rights Approaches

The Capabilities Approach is closely allied with the international human rights movement. Indeed, my version of the approach is characterized as a species of human rights approach. Sen also emphasizes the close link between capabilities and human rights. The common ground between the Capabilities Approach and human rights approaches lies in the idea that all people have some core entitlements just by virtue of their humanity, and that it is a basic duty of society to respect and support these entitlements. (My approach holds that nonhuman animals also have entitlements; to that extent it is broader than the human rights approach.) There is also a close relationship of content. The capabilities on my list overlap substantially with the human rights recognized in the Universal Declaration and other human rights instruments. In effect they cover the same terrain as that of the so-called first-generation rights (political and civil rights) and the so-called second-generation rights (economic and social rights). And they play a similar role, providing a basis both for cross-cultural comparisons and for constitutional guarantees. To the extent that the human rights paradigm has been criticized for being insufficiently attentive to issues of gender, race, and so on, the Capabilities Approach, like the best human rights approaches, tries to remedy those defects.

In some important ways the Capabilities Approach supplements the standard human rights approaches, not least by its philosophical explicitness and clarity about the basic notions involved and by the appeal of its specific formulations. For example, the approach grounds rights claims in bare human birth and minimal agency, not in rationality or any other specific property, something that permits it to recognize the equal human rights of people with cognitive disabilities. It articulates more clearly than most standard rights accounts the relationship between human rights and human dignity (Central Capabilities being defined in part in terms of dignity). It articulates clearly the relationship between human entitlements and those of other species (all sentient beings have entitlements grounded in justice, and tragic conflicts should be solved as they are within a single species, by working for a world in which those conflicts will not occur). Finally, it spells out the relationship between human rights and duties. Human rights approaches are not fully integrated theories; the Capabilities Approach tries to be that.

There is a conceptual connection between the idea of the Central Capabilities as fundamental human entitlements and the idea of duties. Even before we can assign the duties to specific people or groups, the existence of an entitlement entails that there are such duties. Domestically, those duties belong in the first instance to the nation's basic political structure, which is responsible for distributing to all citizens an adequate threshold amount of all entitlements. But poor nations cannot meet all their capability obligations without aid from richer nations. Richer nations consequently have such duties of aid. Other duties to promote human capabilities are assigned to corporations, international agencies and agreements, and, finally, the individual (see Chapter 6).

In my view, there is a conceptual connection between Central Capabilities and government. If a capability really belongs on the list of Central Capabilities, it is because it has an intimate relationship to the very possibility of a life in accordance with human dignity. A standard account of the purposes of government holds that the job of government is, at a minimum, to make it possible for people to live such a life. Other capabilities may be less central to that very possibility, and those may not be the job of government, but government is accountable for the presence of the ten capabilities on my list, if the nation is to be even minimally just. (Of course governments may delegate a portion of this task to private entities, but in the end it is government, meaning the society's basic political structure, that bears the ultimate responsibility for securing capabilities.) When, in the case of the world as a whole, we judge that a single overarching government may not be the best way of solving problems of capability failure, governments still play a major role in securing them: the governments of each nation, in the first place, and, in the second place, the governments of richer nations, which have obligations to assist the poorer nations.

Sen, contrasting human rights with capabilities, remarks that capabilities do not have the conceptual connection to government that human rights clearly do. Sen, however, is speaking of capabilities very generally, not of the Central Capabilities, a concept that he does not use. In many of his writings he seems willing to assess governments in accordance with their performance in delivering capabilities—for example, health care and education—which are central elements on my list. It would appear that we have no major disagreement on this score—or, to the extent that we do, it is part of a more general disagreement about the role that a list of capabilities might play in framing a theory of justice.

The Capabilities Approach in these ways supplements the standard human rights model. It also, however, offers criticisms of at least some familiar versions of that model. One prominent idea of rights, common in the U.S. political and legal tradition, understands rights to be barriers against interfering state action: if the state just keeps its hands off, rights are taken to have been secured. The Capabilities Approach, by contrast, insists that all entitlements involve an affirmative task for government: it must actively support people's capabilities, not just fail to set up obstacles. In the absence of action, rights are mere words on paper. Vasanti was not beaten by the government of Gujarat; she was beaten by her husband. But a government that does not make and then actively enforce laws against domestic violence, or give women the education and skills they need to get a living wage if they leave an abusive marriage, is accountable for the indignity such a woman endures. Fundamental rights are only words unless and until they are made real by government action. The very idea of "negative liberty," often heard in this connection, is an incoherent idea: all liberties are positive, meaning liberties *to do* or *to be* something; and all require the inhibition of interference by others. This is a point that must be emphasized particularly in the United States, where people sometimes imagine that government does its job best when it is inactive.

The difference between "negative" rights and true combined capabilities becomes particularly clear when we consider groups that have long suffered subordination and exclusion. When India was preparing a constitution full of statements about the fundamental rights of citizens, Nehru's law minister B. R. Ambedkar, himself a *dalit* (formerly called "untouchable"), repeatedly pointed out that the assertion of equal rights meant nothing for the excluded unless accompanied by a range of positive state programs to ensure that they could enjoy their rights: prevention of interference by others; economic support so that people would not forgo their rights out of desperation; affirmative action in politics and education. In the absence of such programs, rights are merely words on paper. For similar reasons, the rectification of racism and sexism in America has required not just formally similar treatment but aggressive government action to end unequal opportunity. Our Supreme Court has repeatedly used the language of capabilities when striking down systems of allegedly "separate-but-equal" treatment, holding that black and white children in segregated schools and women denied admission to all-male facilities suffer from capability failure. Courts have repeatedly scrutinized such arrangements by asking what people are really able to do and to be.

 One place where ideas of state inaction and "negative liberty" have been especially pernicious is in the state's relationship to the household or family. The classic liberal distinction between the public and the private spheres aids the natural standoffishness that many liberal thinkers have had about state action: even if it's fine in some areas for the state to act to secure people's rights, there is one privileged sphere that it should not touch, that of the home. Women have rightly complained that some traditional human rights models have wrongly neglected abuses that women suffer in the home. The Capabilities Approach corrects this error, insisting that intervention in the home is justified whenever the rights of its members are violated.

For related reasons, the approach rejects the distinction, common in the human rights movement, between "first-generation rights" (political and civil rights) and "second-generation rights" (economic and social rights). This distinction suggests that political and civil rights do not have economic and social preconditions. The Capabilities Approach insists that they do. All entitlements require affirmative government action, including expenditure, and thus all, to some degree, are economic and social rights.

Sen has argued that the notion of capabilities is broader than the notion of rights, because capabilities can include matters of procedure (whether one is able to engage in a certain sort of process), whereas rights are always matters of substantive opportunity (what one is actually able to have). I think this distinction will not stand up to a scrutiny of the use of rights language in the world's major constitutional traditions. Fundamental rights are often procedural: for example, the right to "due process of law" and the "equal protection of the laws" in the U.S. Constitution (and similar provisions in most modern constitutions). These are fundamental rights, and they are rights to fair procedure. The notion of capabilities is broader than the notion of (human) rights for a different reason: some capabilities are trivial, and some are even bad. The list of Central Capabilities, evaluated as both good and very significant, corresponds closely to the lists of human rights that are standardly defended.

With these corrections in place, the Capabilities Approach can embrace the language of rights and the main conclusions of the international human rights movement, as well as the content of many international human rights documents. The language of rights remains relevant and important. It emphasizes the idea of a fundamental entitlement grounded in the notion of basic justice. It reminds us that people have justified and urgent claims to certain types of treatment, no matter what the world around them has done about that. Even in pursuit of the greatest total or average GDP, or the greatest total or average utility, we may not violate those claims.

4

Fundamental Entitlements

Freedom and Content

The earliest and still most common use of the Capabilities Approach is to supply a new account of the right way to compare and rank development achievements. When nations or regions compete with one another for ranking in the global development "marketplace," trying to show that they offer a better quality of life than other nations do, or than they themselves used to do, the Capabilities Approach provides a new account of the right way to make such comparisons: instead of looking at GNP alone, we must look at a group of central human capabilities. Any capability may in principle serve as a standard of comparison, but in the forging of the Human Development Reports, special attention was given to health and education.

A related use of the approach is to provide a new account of the space of comparison where questions of *equality* are at issue. Equality is usually taken to be an important political value in at least some areas of life. We must then ask, "equality of what?" In debate with opponents who defend the claims of welfare (satisfaction) and resources (income and wealth), Sen has argued that capabilities provide a more attractive benchmark of comparison. His arguments against the alternative views are the same as those that commend capabilities as the right space of comparison in the development debate.

Sen typically focuses on the comparative use of capabilities. At the same time, however, when he assesses real societies he singles out certain capabilities as more important than others: health, education, political participation, nondiscrimination on the basis of race, religion, and gender. He clearly takes an interest in the use of capabilities to define a notion of basic justice. Although he has not presented a formal or enumerated account of capabilities in this connection, he offers many hints of the directions in which his account would go.

By contrast, Sen sometimes speaks as if all capabilities were valuable zones of freedom and as if the overall social task might be to maximize freedom. He speaks of a "perspective of freedom"—as if freedom were a general, all-purpose social good of which the valued capabilities were simply instances. The Nussbaum version of the approach does not proceed in this way. It makes commitments as to content, using the list of ten Central Capabilities as a basis for the idea of fundamental political entitlements and constitutional law.

This task of selection is crucial if the approach is to have anything to say about *justice*. From the point of view of Vasanti's life, some capabilities are of central importance: for example, the freedom of a person to speak, to learn, to participate in politics, to defend her body against assault. Other capabilities that people sometimes make a fuss over seem trivial by comparison: the freedom to ride a motorcycle without a helmet, the freedom not to wear a seat belt. Still others, much coveted by the powerful, may be very bad for the way in which they permit the powerful to inflict harm on others. Many men resent laws against domestic violence and sexual harassment, claiming that such laws interfere with their freedom. A Capabilities Approach that is concerned with justice should not heed such complaints. My version of the approach uses the idea of capabilities as the core of an account of minimal social justice and constitutional law. It therefore needs to defend a specific list of Central Capabilities. In the process, I articulate political principles that can be used as the basis for framing a set of fundamental constitutional entitlements, and the approach I support thus has a close link to law and nation-building.

Why, though, should we not accept Sen's solution: speak of freedom as an overall good and leave to each nation the task of selecting the specific capabilities its constitutional structure will protect? Isn't that sort of approach more respectful of people's democratic choices? Of course I agree that we should not impose anything on democratic nations from without: my proposal is intended for persuasion, and the issue of implementation is a distinct one. The question must be, Why should we try to justify a single set of capabilities in the international arena, arguing that they are important for all nations? Why not, instead, simply commend the general idea of freedom?

First of all, it is unclear whether the idea of promoting freedom is even a coherent political project. Some freedoms limit others. The freedom of rich people to make large donations to political campaigns can limit the equal worth of the right to vote. The freedom of industry to pollute the environment limits the freedom of citizens to enjoy an unpolluted environment. Obviously these freedoms are not among those that Sen considers, but he says nothing to limit the account of freedom or to rule out such conflicts. Indeed, we can go further; the very idea of freedom involves the idea of constraint:

for person P is not free to do action A unless other people are prevented from interfering.

Furthermore, even if there were a coherent project that viewed all freedoms as desirable social goals, it is not at all clear that this is the sort of project someone with the political and ethical aims of the Capabilities Approach ought to endorse. As the examples just given show, any political project that is going to protect the equal worth of certain basic liberties for the poor and to improve their living conditions needs to say forthrightly that some freedoms are central for political purposes, and some are distinctly not. Some freedoms involve basic social entitlements, and others do not. Some lie at the heart of a view of political justice, and others do not. Among the ones that do not lie at the core, some are simply less important, but others may be positively bad.

Gender justice cannot be successfully pursued without limiting male freedom. For example, the "right" to have intercourse with one's wife whether she consents or not has been understood as a cherished male prerogative in most societies, and many men have greatly resented the curtailment of liberty that followed from laws against marital rape—one reason that about half of U.S. states still do not treat nonconsensual intercourse within marriage as genuine rape, and why many societies the world over still lack laws against it. The freedom to harass women in the workplace is a cherished prerogative of males the world over: the minute that sexual harassment regulations are introduced, one always hears protests invoking the idea of liberty. Terms like "femi-nazis" are used to suggest that feminists are against freedom because they support these policies. And of course in one sense feminists are indeed insisting on a restriction of liberty, on the grounds that certain freedoms are inimical both to equalities and to women's liberties and opportunities.

In short, no society that pursues equality or even an ample social minimum can avoid curtailing freedom in very many ways, and what it ought to say is: those freedoms are not good, they are not part of a core group of entitlements required by the notion of social justice, and in many ways, indeed, they subvert those core entitlements. Of other freedoms, for example the freedom of motorcyclists to drive without helmets, they can say, these freedoms are not very important; they are neither very bad nor very good. They are not implicit in our conception of social justice, and certainly they should not appear in a list of fundamental constitutional rights.

If it is true that a society is not minimally just unless it has given people the preconditions of a life worthy of human dignity, then it is incumbent on political actors to figure out what that life requires. If they are to deliver it, they need to know what it is. It seems urgently important to distinguish items that are genuinely fundamental (the freedom of speech, protection of bodily integrity) from items that are not fundamental, and even bad. Legislators, courts, and administrative agencies cannot enforce such a conception unless they know what it is. A written constitution is one handy way of making such entitlements explicit and giving them security against majority whim. Some nations work, instead, with unwritten understandings of fundamental rights. Nonetheless, if they can be removed in an hour by an impatient majority—as the freedoms of speech and association were voted away during the State of Emergency declared by Indira Gandhi in 1975—then human dignity is in a perilous position, and the nation needs to find a better way of delivering *capability security*. Supramajoritarian protection of some type for fundamental entitlements—whether in a written constitution or not—seems essential to that security.

In other words, all societies that pursue a reasonably just political conception have to evaluate human freedoms, saying that some are central and some trivial, some good and some actively bad, some deserving of special protection and others not. This evaluation also affects the way we will assess an abridgment of a freedom. Certain freedoms are taken to be entitlements of citizens based upon justice. When any one of these is abridged, that is an especially grave failure of the political system. In such cases, people feel that the abridgment is not just a cost to be borne; it is a cost of a distinctive kind, involving a violation of basic justice. When some freedom outside the core is abridged, that may be a small cost or a large cost to some actor or actors, but it is not a cost of exactly that same kind, one that in justice no citizen should be asked to bear. An abridgment of the freedom of religion is a cost involving a question of basic entitlement; the abridgment of the freedom to ride on a motorcycle without a helmet does not raise such fundamental issues, although many people may think it a cost.

Sen defends his open-ended way of working with the idea of capabilities by citing the importance of democratic deliberation. My approach also respects the importance of democratic deliberation, in the area of implementation (nothing is imposed on a nation by other nations, except in the most unusual and grave of circumstances) and in the area of concrete specification (each nation specifies each capability in its own way, and, within certain limits, the approach says that this is justified). But it also recognizes that in a working democracy, deliberation takes place at several levels and in many distinct contexts. Citizens can deliberate about the fundamental political principles for which they want their nation to stand—if they are framing a new constitution, for example. Once they have done that, they typically entrench certain entitlements, putting them beyond the reach of change by a simple majority. When such founding documents are unclear or when legislation seems to violate them, courts typically deliberate about the proper interpretation of central entitlements. (Judicial review is a crucial type of democratic deliberation, as virtually every modern democracy recognizes.) Citizens also deliberate about constitutional amendments, and that deliberation is different from the initial framing, since it presupposes a given architecture and some underlying principles, and tinkers with those. And citizens deliberate about legislation—subject to the intervention of courts, if a statute violates constitutional guarantees.

The capabilities list can play a role at any level in this process. It can be used as a source of political principles during a constitutional framing or as a source for interpretation later. It can illuminate judicial interpretation of fundamental entitlements, though within limits set by constitutional text and precedent. It can spur the amendment process: the new constitutional amendment in India protecting a universal right to primary and secondary education was prompted by court cases that recognized the relationship between education and human dignity. Finally, it can be a source of legislation implementing an entitlement. In all these areas deliberation operates. The only way in which the approach cuts off deliberation is that it urges that fundamental entitlements be secured beyond the whim of temporary majority preferences. The process of constitutional amendment ought to be time-consuming and difficult, in order to protect capability security. But that course has been followed by virtually all modern democracies.

There is another, different reason for a theory of justice to take a stand on content. This reason derives from a commitment to political liberalism. If we are convinced that the political principles of a decent society ought to be respectful of a wide range of different comprehensive doctrines and should seek to become the object of an overlapping consensus among them, then we will not want to propose principles that use the idea of capability as a comprehensive theory of the value or quality of life. Theorizing about the overall quality of life should be left to each comprehensive doctrine, using whatever terms and concepts it uses. What it is reasonable to ask citizens to affirm is the political importance of a relatively short and circumscribed list of fundamental entitlements—in the form of the capabilities list—that could be attached to the rest of their comprehensive doctrine in each case. From this perspective Sen's approach—which at times might appear to use capability as a comprehensive index of life value—seems to say too much (whereas the previous argument found it saying too little).

Before considering the Capabilities Approach as a normative political theory, we must at least mention the whole issue of "ideal theory." In his new book on justice, Sen criticizes the whole project of theorizing about justice in a way that sets taxing and somewhat idealized goals. He argues that ideal theory (Rawls being his particular target) is an impediment to thinking well about the options we have before us in real situations: we should favor approaches that rank alternatives comparatively, rather than those that set ideal benchmarks.

This is not the place to assess Sen's critique of Rawls and of ideal theory in general. It is difficult in any case to determine the extent to which those criticisms apply to the version of ideal theory developed in my normative Capabilities Approach, which defends a minimum threshold of capability as a necessary condition for social justice. That approach is not ideal in the sense of being unworldly or utopian, but neither (I believe) is Rawls's approach. This entire issue must be left for future discussion.

Political Justification

The Capabilities Approach—in both its comparative and its normative version—brings moral philosophy into development economics, and this is already progress. Things will go better than they have in the past, Sen and I argue, if development practitioners simply pause to ask tough questions about ethical norms and standards of justice. Even if they don't choose the capability theory in the end, they will be examining ethical norms rather than assuming that these don't matter. The normative version of the approach that I develop in *Women and Human Development* and *Frontiers of Justice* forces even more critical thinking, since it asks people to consider what makes for a minimally just society. Asking that question is already progress, if the baseline is, as is so often the case, ethically heedless decision-making.

But the approach does not leave things at that. It also develops specific arguments against the most common theories of social justice known within moral philosophy. That specific confrontation is part of the process of justification for a normative moral/political view, as I understand it.

The overall account of political justification I defend is based upon John Rawls's account of the method of justification in ethics (which is based, in turn, upon the procedures of Socrates and Aristotle). Like his approach, it uses the name "reflective equilibrium" as the goal of the process of scrutiny. Like Rawls, I view the process as a Socratic attempt to attain clarity about the structure of one's own moral judgments in the area of social justice. Like Rawls again, I view this process as taking on, in politics, a multivocal character: justification is achieved not by individuals acting alone but by debate among Socratically deliberating individuals.

What individuals do, in this process, is to bring to the surface their most secure ethical judgments about justice (Rawls uses the example "slavery is wrong"), and to confront these with a range of theoretical views. The aim is to find a stable fit between judgments and theoretical principles. Nothing is held fixed: an initially compelling judgment may be modified because it conflicts with the deliverances of a theory that has many other advantages; and an initially attractive theory may be rejected because it fails to preserve enough of the most basic judgments. Equilibrium may never be finally achieved, since new theories may remain to be considered. Over time, however, one may hope to have deepened and made more adequate the overall understanding of justice, even if that understanding remains incomplete.

The holder of a theoretical view must begin by outlining the arguments that generate it, trying to make a *prima facie* case for the view by showing that it does square with some very powerful ethical intuitions and judgments. This I do by arguing that the ten capabilities are important components of the idea of a life in accordance with human dignity. Like Rawls, I view my arguments as essentially Socratic in character: I appeal to the interlocutor to ponder what is implicit in the notion of human dignity and a life in accordance with it. I ask the interlocutor to consider that certain ways of life that human beings are forced to lead are not fully human, in the sense of being not worthy of the dignity of the human being. I believe that this intuitive starting point offers definite, albeit highly general, guidance. Marx's vivid descriptions of forms of labor that allow continued life, but not a fully human life, resonate the world over. The notion of a life in accordance with human dignity is one of the most fertile ideas used in worldwide constitutional jurisprudence. So I argue, in a very general and intuitive way, moving through various areas of life influenced by public policy, that the protection of these ten basic entitlements is an essential requirement of life with human dignity.

Like Rawls, I attempt to show that the approach offers a good basis for political principles in a pluralistic society, by demonstrating that it could, over time, become the basis for an "overlapping consensus" among holders of the main religious and secular views (the major religions and the major secular ethical views, such as Kantian or pragmatist views). The approach, then, is a form of "political liberalism," showing respect for citizens by not asking them to endorse a political doctrine built on any particular religious or metaphysical view. Overlapping consensus is not a current reality, of course (nor does Rawls require this). One need only show that over time it is plausible to imagine that it might become a reality. Imagining this transition is especially difficult for the part of the view that defends animal entitlements. It seems to me, however, that even there overlapping consensus is ultimately plausible.

This argument, however, is only a preliminary: for at this point the reader may think there are quite a few other views that offer similar advantages. Here, then, the Capabilities Approach begins to confront the major opponents from the theoretical tradition, trying to show that they do not do as well, at least in some respects. In comparison with informed-desire utilitarianism and the classical theory of the social contract, the Capabilities Approach has at least some advantages. It also squares reasonably well, however, with the best version of such approaches.

Before examining these two theoretical alternatives more closely, we need to say more about how empirical material regarding poor people's actual efforts and struggles figures in the approach. What about Vasanti's story, for example? I have used it here in a primarily illustrative way, to clarify what the Capabilities Approach offers by contrast with the other approaches known in the development world. I have also mentioned that it seems an advantage, other things equal, that the approach asks a question that real people like Vasanti ask and answer: an approach that does so cannot be accused of being a purely Western construct.

But of course the arguments for the approach do not rely simply on stories and examples: they use abstract notions (the idea of human dignity, the idea of a capability) and abstract philosophical arguments. They also defend capabilities that Vasanti might not have defended: the freedom of the press, for example, can be defended as important to poor people in a democracy, even if they themselves do not talk about it a lot or feel that they want it.

More generally, the Capabilities Approach is not based upon subjective preferences, although it takes preferences seriously. It argues strongly against preference-based approaches within development economics and within philosophy. It views preferences as often unreliable for political purposes. Only the most fully corrected informed-desire approaches play even a subsidiary role in political justification. Vasanti's story and other such stories obviously do not even supply a comprehensive account of people's preferences—that must come from other, empirical materials. They could not supply a justification, because no subjective materials can supply that. What role, then, do such stories play?

The role they played for me was primarily educational: without seeing a wide range of conditions within which women like Vasanti work and strive, I might well have missed important problems, or missed their connections to one another. Readers may be in a similar position. The idea that education is linked to the ability to protect bodily integrity by exiting an abusive marriage, for example, might not be obvious to a scholar ruminating in a very different society. Such detailed examples can also be educative for the reader, who might not be able to imagine such different life-conditions without the help of narrative. Narratives help such readers focus on a wider range of problems and issues, and also cultivate the imagination, producing an acknowledgment of the equal humanity of people whose lives typically are ignored by privileged elites. Examples also clarify the theoretical argument by showing exactly how two positions differ.

Informed-Desire Welfarism

Although we have already seen how the Capabilities Approach differs from the simple version of utilitarianism used by many development economists, more needs to be said to show how the approach is different from, and superior to, the more sophisticated forms of utilitarianism known within philosophy, particularly views that acknowledge that existing preferences are often deformed and offer numerous corrections to them.

Such views typically ask what people's preferences would be if they had full and comprehensive information, a useful corrective. It is reasonable to describe such views as basically "welfarist," that is, based on people's preferences about their welfare, so long as we can say, "Now we have arrived at people's real, or authentic, preferences: for surely the preferences they would have under full information are more truly theirs than the preferences they have under misinformation."

Such theories, however, typically introduce a variety of other corrections that are more difficult to square with pure welfarism. By closely examining three of the most sophisticated such views, those of economist John Harsanyi and philosophers Richard Brandt and Jean Hampton, I argue in *Women and Human Development* that these theorists cannot generate results that seem to them to be just without introducing moral notions that are independent of people's preferences. Thus their views are ultimately mixed views, not pure forms of welfarism.

Harsanyi identifies a certain class of preferences as "sadistic or malicious," that is, involving pleasure in the pain or subordination of others. He does not doubt that these are genuine preferences of people that may be deep-seated; they could not be removed by more or better information. In that sense, they are people's real preferences. Harsanyi, however, simply leaves such preferences out of account. He announces that he is doing so in order to combine the utilitarian reliance on preferences with a Kantian idea of a community of equals and with Adam Smith's idea of the impartial spectator. His view, then, is only in part a form of welfarism.

Brandt is not so straightforward about his departures from welfarism, but we can show that although he claims to use a value-free method of winnowing preferences, he actually employs some controversial values, such as independence from authority and autonomy, in the process of deciding which preferences are "authentic." He cannot plausibly claim that these norms are a part of every human being's personality, so he has not shown that these are the preferences that each person would have under ideal conditions. In this and other ways he incorporates independent moral notions into his theory.

Jean Hampton, focusing on the difficulties that preference-based views confront when we think of women's deformed preferences in abusive or asymmetrical relationships, proposes corrections involving equal respect and nonintimidation: the preferences that count are the ones people would have if they lived in such conditions. These corrections seem to go to the heart of the matter, making the results even more adequate than those of Harsanyi and Brandt from the point of view of social justice. As Hampton acknowledges, however, they are not generated from within a preference-based account. Equal respect is not a part of many people's personalities, and the desire to intimidate others, unfortunately, may go very deep. By introducing these constraints, then, we are not simply discovering what people would prefer under conditions of full information.

The authors of all these views, in order to generate results that they consider morally acceptable, have departed from utilitarianism and have incorporated some of the key moral elements of the Capabilities Approach: the idea of equal human dignity, the idea that practical reason is a very important capability, the idea that people should not have the right to remove the fundamental entitlements of others.

Are these corrected views as satisfactory as the Capabilities Approach once we incorporate those independent constraints? I believe not. All utilitarian views—even with some independent constraints—still involve aggregation across heterogeneous elements of lives, and all involve a commitment to pursuing the best social total, or average. Thus even the more sophisticated views do not escape the problems identified earlier in the versions of utilitarianism used in development economics. Finally, none adequately addresses the problem of adaptive preferences. It is possible to winnow preferences by adding information, or by simply dropping preferences that have sadistic or malicious elements. But, as Elster and Sen have both argued, it is just not possible to correct the problem of adaptation, because it involves people's entire upbringing in a society. Adaptation is not just lack of information. If women have learned that education is not for women, they will not easily change on account of new information about the benefits and pleasures of education. Some will, but not those who have deeply internalized the idea that a proper woman does not go in for schooling. At the same time, it is not possible to identify the preferences that represent adaptation to an unjust or wrongly hierarchical state of affairs—without an independent theory of social justice, which the utilitarian approach refuses to give us. Even the corrected views, then, retain some serious problems.

Utilitarianism has many defects, but it has the great merit of taking people and their desires seriously and showing respect for what people want. Some ethical views, particularly those in the Kantian tradition, dismiss desire prematurely, treating it as a brutish and utterly unintelligent part of the personality. I argue against those views, suggesting that desire is an intelligent interpretive aspect of the personality that is sensitive to information about the good: thus informed desires, of the sort that are the focus of the best such views (those, like Harsanyi's and Hampton's, with independent moral constraints built in), still play some important roles in political justification. Desire can help us ascertain whether the view we favor is likely to be stable, and showing that a view can be stable is part of justifying it as an acceptable political view.

Social Contract Views

More recently, my own view has also taken on the powerful theories of justice long developed within the social contract tradition, beginning with John Locke in the seventeenth century. Although the important theory of justice produced by John Rawls offers a powerful theoretical account of social distribution in many areas, it appropriates some assumptions from the classical Lockean theory of the social contract that Rawls himself saw as raising difficulties for his theory in four areas. The areas of difficulty that Rawls identified are justice for future generations; justice across national boundaries; the fair treatment of people with disabilities; and moral issues involved in our treatment of nonhuman animals (which Rawls, unlike me, did not see as raising issues of justice). Rawls himself solved the first problem reasonably well, with his "just savings principle." (Similar ideas have yet to be explicitly integrated into the Capabilities Approach.) He attempted to solve the second in his last book, *The Law of Peoples*, but I believe that attempt was not very successful. The last two, which he saw as issues on which his view might "fail," reveal serious weaknesses in his theory and cannot be solved without a more radical modification of the theory than he himself was willing to make. Those three problem areas are the three "frontiers" that I identify in my book *Frontiers of Justice*. If we are to pursue the issues that lie at these frontiers, we must consider an alternative to Rawls's theory, though without rejecting its insights.

Rawls's theory has a mixed intellectual pedigree. Most of its difficulties (from the point of view of the Capabilities Approach) come from the fact that it is a descendant of the classical theory of the social contract. It also incorporates Kantian ethical elements, for example, the idea that each person is an end and not a means, and these elements greatly enrich it. However, at the end of the day Rawls was unwilling to drop the social contract structure in favor of a more purely Kantian theory. Nor is the Kantian strand in Rawls utterly free from difficulty. In the area of justice for people with disabilities, the Kantian elements themselves prove problematic, because Kant grounds respect on a high degree of moral rationality and thus is unable to accord fully equal respect to people with severe cognitive disabilities. Let us now, however, pursue the difficulties associated with the social contract tradition.

The classical theory of the social contract begins from the observation that all existing social structures have been dictated by artificial hierarchies of wealth, class, and prestige. If we strip human beings of all those artificial advantages, the theory asks, what sort of society would they choose? This thought experiment is enormously valuable, and Rawls's famous Original Position is one version of it: rational individuals are asked to select principles of justice for society in ignorance of their class, wealth, race, and sex. However, in the process of designing the thought experiment (which is supposed to show us something about how institutions could respect the humanity that we equally share, despite the artificial advantages that divide us), all contract theories, including Rawls's, assume a rough equality of physical and mental power among the participants. It is precisely that awareness of a rough equality (even the weakest can kill the strongest by stealth) that convinces the parties that they will not be able to dominate others securely, and that it is therefore in their mutual advantage to surrender some of their natural assets and to agree to political and legal constraints. The theory maintains that the contract is to the mutual advantage of the participants; it is advantage, not altruism or love of others, that brings them together in society. (Of course such theories don't maintain that real people lack beneficence: the theory develops a hypothetical representation; it is not writing history or anthropology. The point is that we needn't assume extensive beneficence in order to show how the contract gets going.)

Such theories give us great insight into social cooperation and social justice. If we agree that justice requires us to treat people impartially, not favoring one person or group over another because of wealth, or class, or other artificial advantages such as race or gender, such theories give us enormous help in seeing what a society built on an ideal of impartiality would look like. Rawls's theory of justice is one of the great achievements of modern Western political philosophy. It solves the set of problems it sets out to solve very well indeed. To show that a rival view does better over the whole range of problems would be a huge task, and one that the Capabilities Approach has not attempted so far.

But the assumptions of rough equality and mutual advantage mean that the view cannot deal well with cases in which we find a deep asymmetry of power between the parties that is not easily corrected by simply rearranging income and wealth. Precisely for that reason, people with severe physical and cognitive disabilities are explicitly omitted from the Original Position and are not included under the definition of the capacities of citizens in the Well Ordered Society. Their needs, says Rawls, are to be dealt with at some point but are not taken into account when society selects its most basic principles and structures. In effect, they are to be dominated, though the domination is to be beneficent. This problem is exacerbated by the fact that Rawls's Kantian conception of the person is based on rationality (both prudential and moral): so people with severe cognitive disabilities just don't count as persons under that view. Rawls explicitly holds that human beings who can't enter into agreements or contracts are not owed political justice. Thus for Rawls the whole issue of justice is moot for at least many people with disabilities.

As for nonhuman animals, Rawls does not believe that our relations with them involve issues of justice, presumably for similar reasons involving their lack of rational capacity. He therefore thinks that we have ethical duties to animals but not political duties. I argue that the presence of any type of agency or striving accompanied by sentience raises questions of justice and makes it appropriate to consider the beings in question subjects of a political theory of justice, whether or not they are capable of understanding or assessing that theory. This difference in the basic account of where and to whom justice is appropriate means that for me it is quite straightforward to conclude that almost all animals (perhaps excluding those with minimal sentience and no movement, such as sponges) are subjects of justice and have a dignity (connected to the characteristic form of agency of their kind) that deserves respect and support from laws and institutions. The Capabilities Approach needs modification to deal with obligations to nonhuman animals, but that modification is straightforward and does not require jettisoning any essential elements of the theory.

The Capabilities Approach has not been shown to be superior to Rawls's version of the social contract in all areas—only in these three problem areas. Much more work would need to be done to show that it was superior overall. Moreover, it is not clear that the core of the Rawlsian approach to justice could not be reformulated in a way that would preserve most of Rawls's essential insights but would meet my criticisms. Henry Richardson has offered such a reformulation—though Richardson acknowledges that it involves changes to Rawls's theory that Rawls himself would never have accepted.

Moreover, as *Frontiers of Justice* insists, there are other types of Kantian contractarianism that do not make the assumptions that I view as problematic in Rawls's theory: Thomas Scanlon's ethical contractarianism, for example. Scanlon proposes that we assess principles by asking whether they could reasonably be rejected by any of the parties involved; he does not assume that the parties are roughly equal in physical and mental capacity, nor that they pursue mutual advantage. His idea is ethical rather than political, and he acknowledges that if it were to become a political idea it would need an account of political goods. If such an account were suitably formulated (for example, in terms of the Central Capabilities, an idea with which Scanlon shows sympathy), it would still be somewhat different in structure from my Capabilities Approach, but it would use the same ideas, since I employ the notion of reasonable rejection, or something very close to it, in articulating my account of political justification. So the social contract tradition in its classical form has been rejected, but its core idea of a fair agreement survives. Just as it seems good to look for a convergence between the best informed-desire theories and the Capabilities Approach, so too here: to the extent that such a contractarian approach delivers results similar to ours, that generates confidence that we are on the right track.

Political Liberalism and Overlapping Consensus

If the Capabilities Approach takes issue with Rawls in some areas, it also endorses and develops another prominent aspect of his approach to political justice: the idea of *political liberalism*. Given that all societies contain a plurality of religious and secular views of the meaning and purpose of human life, it seems strategically unwise to adopt a political view that opts for one of these against the others: such a political regime is likely to prove unstable, at least under conditions of freedom. But that is not the only or even the primary objection to that sort of political doctrine. The deeper moral problem is that any such doctrine is insufficiently respectful of citizens who hold a different view. Such views are worst when they repress dissent, for example, or set up conditions of orthodoxy that attach to a person's ability to hold office. But even a benign religious (or anti-religious) establishment threatens equality by creating an in-group and a variety of out-groups. It says that all citizens do not enter the public square on equal terms. Equal respect for persons seems to require government to avoid taking a stand, wherever possible, on the religious and metaphysical issues that divide citizens along the lines of their comprehensive doctrines (meaning overall approaches to value and meaning in life, whether religious or secular).

Of course a political view must take a moral stand, basing political principles on some definite values, such as impartiality and equal respect for human dignity. Such values, however, either are or can become a part of the many comprehensive doctrines that citizens reasonably hold. If they are articulated in a calculatedly "thin" way, without grounding in controversial metaphysical notions (such as the idea of the immortal soul), epistemological notions (such as the idea of self-evident truth), or thicker ethical doctrines (such as Kantianism or Aristotelianism), they can potentially command the approval of a wide range of citizens subscribing to different religious and secular positions. What is asked of them is that they endorse the basic ideas of the Capabilities Approach *for political purposes only*, not as a comprehensive guide to life, and that they view them as operative within a distinctive domain, namely, that of the political. Endorsement here does not simply mean that the person grudgingly grants that we have to live by these ideas. Endorsement means that the person really holds these ideas—*as one part* of her overall view of how to live. (Rawls uses the image of a "module" that can be attached to the rest of a person's comprehensive doctrine.)

Neither Rawls nor I holds that such an "overlapping consensus" on basic political principles (the principles of justice in his case, the Capabilities Approach in mine) must already be present in society.

We require only that there be a plausible path to that endorsement, such that, over time, it is not unreasonable to suppose that society could arrive at that consensus. Nor does overlapping consensus require the suppression of people who think differently. In any society there will be those who cannot accept some aspects of the political doctrine that governs it—who oppose equal voting rights for women, for example, or who favor racial segregation. Such people may go on living in the society and may speak their mind freely, so long as they do not violate the rights of others or cause an imminent risk of violent disorder. If their numbers were very large, their presence would threaten the stability of the political system and its constitution. Rawls and I both believe that we can show, however, that most of the major comprehensive doctrines in modern societies could, over time, come to support the principles we endorse.

If we include in the political view a strong defense of animal entitlements, the emergence of consensus becomes a long-range project. Even here, however, I believe that a consensus on a threshold of decent living conditions for animals can emerge.

One area in which ideas of overlapping consensus and equal respect have special importance is that of religion and its relation to the state. The capabilities list gives religious liberty a prominent place, but it does not describe the type of protection for religion that is compatible with the basic idea of equal respect for human dignity. It is, however, possible to say quite a lot more about this question, and I have tried to do so in *Liberty of Conscience*. I believe that equal respect for people's dignity requires ample free-exercise protections, including space for what U.S. law calls "accommodations": that is, exemptions, for minorities, to general laws that burden their conscience; exemptions, for example, to laws concerning work days, drug use, and compulsory military service. I also argue that the idea of equal respect is difficult if not impossible to render compatible with any type of religious establishment, even one that is benign and noncoercive. Any established church (or the governmental imposition of secularism) denigrates nonbelievers in the favored doctrine by stating that they are an out-group.

Realizing an equal-respect conception of religious capability is a delicate matter, requiring sensitivity to many contextual and historical factors that shape the social meaning of governmental choices. Studying the ways in which different nations have pursued this general goal gives us insight into what it means to realize a capability through law (and, thus, through a combination of legislative and judicial action). This type of study should, in principle, be performed for every capability in every country, and the capabilities should ultimately be studied, not in isolation, but in their network of relations to other capabilities. (For of course the capabilities are not isolated units; they are a set of opportunities that shape one another and that must ultimately be realized as a total set.) Thus *Liberty of Conscience* is the first step in a huge research program. The more we carry it out, the more confident we can be in arguing that the Capabilities Approach can become, over time, the object of an overlapping consensus in a pluralistic society.

Because the Capabilities Approach, as developed in *Women and Human Development* and *Frontiers of Justice,* is a form of political liberalism, it is not a comprehensive doctrine of any sort. It is therefore mistaken, and a serious misreading of my political views, to call it a form of *cosmopolitanism.* Although the approach includes an account of global as well as domestic justice, it is simply wrong to identify it with the comprehensive ethical theory known as "cosmopolitanism," which is usually defined as the view that one's first loyalty should be to humanity as a whole rather than to one's nation, region, religion, or family. Cosmopolitans can probably accept most of what I recommend, but one does not have to be a cosmopolitan to accept the idea that all citizens (in one's nation, and then, in a second step, in all nations) should have a minimum threshold amount of the ten capabilities. Most of the major comprehensive doctrines, religious and secular, I argue, can accept that idea, and few of them could accept a comprehensive cosmopolitanism. To give just one example, Roman Catholic social doctrine squares quite well with the global and domestic demands of the Capabilities Approach, but no orthodox Roman Catholic can be a cosmopolitan, since cosmopolitanism asserts that my *first* duty is to all humanity rather than to God or my religion. Whether my own comprehensive ethical doctrine is cosmopolitan or not is a separate question (it isn't, but it is close). The point that is relevant here is that the Capabilities Approach is a political doctrine only, and one that aspires to be the object of an Overlapping Consensus. As such, it should not recommend any comprehensive ethical doctrine or be built upon one. Calling it a form of cosmopolitanism is tantamount to saying that it does not respect the diversity of religious and secular doctrines that all modern nations contain. But respecting that plurality is a central aim of my theoretical approach.

Consequentialism and Deontology

Philosophical approaches in ethics and politics are usually divided (sometimes overly simply) into two groups. Consequentialist approaches are those that assess the goodness of an option by asking whether, and to what extent, it maximizes the best consequences (and they then offer some account of what good consequences are). In other words, they start with a conception of what is good and define right choice in terms of that. Deontological views are those that start from a conception of duty or right action and permit the pursuit of the good only within the constraints of the right. Thus Kant allows the moral agent to pursue happiness—but only within the constraints of a morality built upon respect and impartiality.

This distinction is rather crude. Deontological views can ascribe a positive value to pursuit of the good, and Kant's view surely does this. Consequentialist views, as Sen has prominently argued, may incorporate into their account of good consequences certain elements that are standardly understood as deontological, such as that rights are preserved. It is not even clear that consequentialism must balance rights against other elements of the good, rather than treating them as mandatory: for the account of the good may be a layered one, with orders of priority (although that is not the sort of account Sen favors).

The Capabilities Approach has close links to deontology. One of its most important historical antecedents is Kant, and it holds that social welfare should never be pursued in a way that violates people's fundamental entitlements. Indeed, it agrees with Kantians in saying that utilitarianism does not attach the right sort of salience to each person and to the idea of respect for persons. The *principle of each person as end* that I make central to the view from *Women and Human Development* onward is a version of Kant's idea of the duty to respect humanity as an end, and never to treat it as a mere means.

The Capabilities Approach also lies close to deontology in its embrace of political liberalism. Consequentialism is typically presented as a comprehensive doctrine: the right choice, anywhere and on any topic, is the choice that maximizes good consequences, as defined in the theory. Consequentialists typically do not distinguish the political domain of life from the rest of life, nor do they limit their recommendations to the political domain. They say that their method of choice is the right one everywhere. They thus make demands of citizens that are unreasonable, from the point of view of political liberalism. Many religious citizens may be perfectly happy to support a society based on the ten capabilities, but be unwilling to grant that the right choice is always one that maximizes good consequences. Their religion may offer a different account of right choice. So if consequentialism is presented, as it standardly is, as a comprehensive view of the right and the good, it could not provide the foundation for political principles in any form of political liberalism, whether that espoused by the Capabilities Approach or some other.

In another way, however, the Capabilities Approach can be seen as a cousin of consequentialism, or even as a form of political, nonwelfarist consequentialism. It announces that the right way to judge whether a given political situation is adequate, from the point of view of justice, is to look at *outcomes:* Are the fundamental entitlements of citizens met, and in a secure way? It thus might be called an *outcome-oriented view,* by contrast to *proceduralist views* that are often preferred by deontologists. John Rawls offers the following illuminating example. Suppose we are dividing a pie, and we want to divide it fairly. One way of thinking about fairness is to look to the outcome of the division: the fair process is the one that gives us equal shares. Another way of thinking about it is to look at procedure: the fair division may be the one in which everyone takes a turn with the knife. Rawls likens his theory to the latter type of division. The Capabilities Approach is an example of the former. When we look at a society and ask, "Is that society minimally just?," we look at whether the capabilities have been secured. Of course there are some capabilities that involve an idea of fair procedure (in the criminal law, a right to a fair trial; in other areas, due process rights of a range of types). But those become part of the good outcome against which society's operations are assessed.

Such an outcome-oriented criterion of justice does not make the Capabilities Approach a form of consequentialism, because it is a *partial* account of specifically political entitlements, not a comprehensive view of the social good. Still, there is a real interest in finding out how well people are actually doing, and in this sense it is reasonable to classify the Capabilities Approach with approaches that focus on promoting social welfare—understanding welfare, of course, in terms of capabilities, not the satisfaction of preferences.

Political Emotions and the Problem of Stability

All political views, especially those that make extensive demands on people, need to show that they can remain stable over time, and stable not just out of grudging acquiescence but out of a well-informed acceptance of the key elements of the view and stable motivations to support it. The Capabilities Approach does not rely on the idea that the social contract will be for the mutual advantage of all its participants, an idea that the classical theory of the social contract used to good effect in explaining why its principles could be expected to be stable. One advantage of setting up the contract in this way was that one did not need to rely on extensive altruism. My view, by contrast, does need to rely on altruism, and therefore needs to have a great deal to say about how and why altruistic motivations arise, what other motivations they must contend with, and how we might cultivate the helpful sentiments in a socially propitious way. India's founders, Gandhi and Nehru, thought long and well about how politicians can build a public culture that puts altruism and the relief of misery at its core. For a time they did so. Today that consensus is fraying. An account of the emotions of citizens in a decent society is urgently needed.

This task involves thinking about the family, about social norms, about schools, and about the ways in which political institutions create incentives. It also requires conceptual thought about the emotions, how they arise and unfold, what their structure is, and how they interact with one another.

Implementation

The Capabilities Approach maps out an ambitious set of goals. But what does it say about how to get there? It certainly insists that all the capabilities on the list are important and that subordinating one to another will not be a recipe for achieving full justice. As we'll see in the final chapter, it also makes some recommendations about constitutional design and institutional structure, although the latter is an area in which much more work is needed. Clearly, one of the major avenues of implementation of the Central Capabilities is a nation's system of constitutional adjudication involving fundamental rights. Finally, the approach reminds policy-makers that the goal is always to present people with choices in the areas the list identifies as central, rather than to dragoon them into a specific mode of functioning. This emphasis on choice certainly shapes the strategies of implementation that policy-makers should consider.

To some extent, further recommendations for implementation should be context-specific. Recipes for moving people above the threshold on the Central Capabilities will probably be useless un-

less they are informed by a detailed knowledge of the cultural, political, and historical context of their choices. (This is why *Women
and Human Development* was written as a book about specific regions
of India, rather than as an account of what women need all over
the world, although some conclusions about the more general question are indeed suggested by my specific studies.) If we return to
Vasanti's story, however, we can see that the guidance the approach
offers goes further. The capabilities are seen not as isolated atoms
but as a set of opportunities that interact and inform one another.
So it makes sense, as Wolff and De-Shalit emphasize, to identify fertile functionings (or rather capabilities): opportunities that generate other opportunities. To some extent, the fertile capabilities will
themselves be context-specific, but it's a good bet that in all nations
education is one of them, providing access not only to employment
options and political voice but also to greater bargaining power in
the household, hence the power to stand up for oneself. Vasanti was
only beginning to be educated when I met her, but it's clear that
the failure of her parents to educate her had held her back for a
long time, and that SEWA's education programs have given many
women like her options they never had before—programs focused
not just on technical skills but also on critical thinking and the
ability to grasp, with imagination and information, the nature of
one's historical and political situation. This is not just a recipe for
people in developing nations: richer nations, too, often fail to educate their poor and deprived citizens, and intervention that focuses
on education can be especially fertile here, too. (Consider the novel
Push, by Sapphire, recently made into the successful and critically
acclaimed movie *Precious:* it shows the tremendous impact of reading on the ability of a woman to cope resourcefully with a life that
has included terrible violence and deprivation, and, indeed, on that

woman's whole sense of herself as a person of dignity and worth, to whom justice is due.)

Another fertile capability in Vasanti's case was ownership: the independence provided by credit. Both credit and landownership have tremendous importance as sources of other capabilities, such as employment opportunities, the capability of protecting one's bodily integrity from domestic violence, and a kind of confidence and self-respect that Vasanti clearly began to enjoy only after the SEWA loan.

Finally, in the groups studied by Wolff and De-Shalit (which, we should remember, are in rich, developed countries), just as in Vasanti's case, an especially fertile capability is that of affiliation: having links to other people (in Vasanti's case, the women of SEWA) who regard them with respect and as equals, and who are determined to care for them and share in common projects with them.

Just as politicians have reason to spend scarce resources on the most fertile capabilities, expecting those to generate improvement in yet other areas, so they have reason to focus their energies on removing what Wolff and De-Shalit call *corrosive disadvantage,* types of capability failure that lead to failure in other areas. Although conceptually corrosive disadvantage is the flip side of fertile capability, it can't always just be read off from an understanding of the fertile capabilities. Racial discrimination and stigma, for example, are a source of corrosive disadvantage that we could not discover simply by studying the capability of affiliation, although it is in some respects a failure of that capability. Similarly, an inability to speak the local language was found by Wolff and De-Shalit to be corrosive, in ways that one might not have predicted if one thought only of education as a generally fertile capability. Each society, then, has reason to try to pinpoint types of disadvantage that seem particularly undermining and to use scarce resources to address these as a top priority. Often these will be failures connected to marginalization, stigma, and other forms of group-based powerlessness, giving societies reason to adopt group-based remedies, even though the end in view is always the full empowerment of each individual.

5

CULTURAL DIVERSITY

The list of Central Human Capabilities is a single list, albeit a very general one that can be further specified in many different ways. Even when used as a comparative measure, the human development paradigm applies the same standards to all nations, ranking them against one another in terms of their ability to deliver to people a range of important human capabilities. Yet we live in a highly diverse world. Isn't it dictatorial or obtuse to apply a single set of norms to all the world's peoples? Doesn't this way of proceeding smack of imperialism? This important question has been at the heart of our work on the approach. As an international team of researchers whose origins lie in a range of both Western and non-Western cultures, we have been aware of a raging debate about the alleged value-imperialism involved in universalism, and we have been extremely concerned to address it.*

---

* Sen, for example, is a Bengali Indian; though he has acquired British citizenship and currently resides in the United States, he retains his Indian citizenship and a profound engagement with Indian politics and culture. I am a U.S. citizen, but my work has led me to India for much of my research, as well as to a variety of other nations. The leading founders

Since the Capabilities Approach is a close relative of the international human rights movement (in my view, one species of it), we would do well to begin by confronting the objections so frequently brought against that movement, before turning to the particular contributions of the Capabilities Approach. It has frequently been said that the human rights movement—the most common and influential form of the view that all human beings everywhere have certain fundamental entitlements—is Western in origin, and that the endorsement of international human rights norms as major human goals thus reinforces the subordination of non-Western cultures to a Western ideology. Having so recently extricated themselves from colonial domination, they are now being colonized anew. What should we make of this argument?

First of all, it is not yet an argument. Even if it were true that human rights are historically Western, that fact by itself does not provide a reason to reject them as unsuitable for other nations. People borrow things all the time, and the resourcefulness with which cultures make use of originally external materials is one of the most significant facts of human history. Moreover, societies sometimes borrow not just little pieces of an external view but large systematic views that originally came from without. All the major cultural movements of the world—including Christianity, Buddhism, Islam, and Marxism—had specific origins in a given place and time but spread widely beyond their original location because people were

---

of the Human Development and Capability Association include researchers with the following nationalities: Pakistani, Japanese, Brazilian, Dutch, Italian, Bangladeshi, British, and American; members are drawn from eighty countries. The presidents of the association have included two Indians, one British citizen, and one U.S. citizen.

drawn to them. There is no reason to see this phenomenon as inherently objectionable. It has rarely been argued that the Western origins of Marxism give non-Western nations a reason not to adopt Marxism. Adopting Marxism might have been a mistake, but not because it got started in the work of a German Jew in the British Library. Some further argument has to be given. There is no more cogency to a similar contention about human rights. Unless we can give some further reason that other cultures should not adopt the concepts involved in the human rights movement, we have not yet said anything of substance.

Even as a thesis about history, however, the "imperialism" charge runs into grave difficulty. As Amartya Sen has shown, the constituent elements of the idea of human rights exist in both Indian and Chinese traditions. They were configured in a particular way in the European Enlightenment (before which the Western philosophical tradition itself had only some elements of the idea), but that fact does not show that the idea, in its deeper structure, is peculiarly Western. Some ideas that we often associate with the Enlightenment actually existed in India long before they existed in the West. The idea of religious toleration, for example, can be found in the thought of the Buddhist emperor Ashoka in the third to second centuries B.C.E.

The modern architects of the international human rights movement, which begins with the formulation of the Universal Declaration of Human Rights in 1948, came from a wide range of nations, including Egypt, China, and France. They deliberately formulated the list in such a way as to make it acceptable to people from a wide range of cultural and religious traditions. More recently, all the major international human rights instruments have been formulated by international teams, with a prominent role for people from non-

Western nations. The United States, which is usually the country whose imperialistic role the objector most fears, has not taken a lead in this movement. Far from it: the United States has not even ratified most of the major human rights instruments, including the Convention on the Elimination of All Forms of Discrimination against Women (CEDAW) and the Convention on the Rights of the Child (CRC), both of which have been ratified by most of the other developing and developed nations of the world.* To suggest that the United States is trying to foist human rights norms on an unwilling world shows gross ignorance.

If we take a closer look at the history of colonialism, moreover, we do not find human rights norms, in colonized nations, emerging from a demand by colonizers that the colonized people accept "Western values." Instead, these norms are much more accurately seen as artifacts of resistance to arbitrary colonial power. Consider India, whose constitution protects human rights very comprehensively. The British Raj did not import to India norms of freedom of speech, freedom of association, and political liberty. Those norms may have been defended back home in some quarters and by some people, for some people; but in ruling India the British showed utter contempt for human rights ideas. Indians could hardly have associated empire with the idea of human rights, when what they endured every day involved mandatory segregation and denial of associational freedom; violent, sometimes murderous, assaults on people attempting to speak and protest freely; arrest and deten-

---

* The nations that have not ratified CEDAW are the United States, Iran, Tonga, Palau, Somalia, Sudan, Niue, and Vatican City (certainly a central source of "Western values"). The CRC has been ratified by every member of the United Nations except the United States and Somalia.

tion without charge or trial; and other offenses too numerous to list. Rabindranath Tagore, the 1913 Nobel Prize–winning poet who returned his knighthood in 1919 to protest British atrocities in violation of human rights, characterized Western culture as built on a foundation of arbitrary power, without respect for humanity. Tagore, who admired many Western thinkers, knew well that there were other currents in Western culture, including ideas of respect and entitlement; but he was making the point that a contempt for rights was currently dominant in Europe's behavior toward the rest of the world.

When, much later, Gandhi and Nehru insisted on building the new Indian nation on a strong foundation of human rights, they did so after having suffered for many years from the constant violation of those rights by the British during the independence struggle. Both, but particularly Nehru, spent long periods in British jails for the "offense" of peaceful protest. Gandhi was no lover of Western culture; like Tagore, he saw it as materialistic and power-driven. He embraced human rights for their intrinsic importance, and he insisted that their foundation could be found, ultimately, in Indian traditions as he interpreted them.

Much the same story might be told about the role of human rights in the framing of the South African constitution. The strongly human rights–based Constitution of the modern nation represents an attempt to codify protections for human dignity so that no future arbitrary regime might violate dignity as it had been violated every day under apartheid. When we consider the extraordinary fact that South Africa's Constitution forbade not only gender and race-based discrimination but also discrimination on grounds of sexual orientation—in 1996, while the United States was upholding the constitutionality of sodomy laws, and long before any other nation had taken serious legal steps in this matter—we can see the extent to which protection of the weak against the tyranny of the strong was at the heart of the Framers' enterprise.

So the "imperialism" objection to human rights falls flat. The human rights agenda upholds the equal worth and dignity of all persons. The idea of equal worth is not especially Western, and it certainly is not imperial. The human rights program is the ally of the weak against the strong.

The "imperialism" objection is, however, very influential in the international development world. If, therefore, we want to avoid making these points again and again, we can draw attention to the fact that the Capabilities Approach, though closely linked to the human rights approach, has its primary origin in India, and its articulation has been the work of an international group of researchers. More important, the Capabilities Approach stays close to the ground. It does not employ, at its core, any highly rarified theoretical concept, such as the idea of "human rights" is sometimes taken to be. Instead, it asks and answers a question that real people pose to themselves and others, in many different contexts, every day of their lives: "What am I able to do and to be? What are my real options?" It's at least possible to contend that people in nation N lack the concept of human rights—although I believe this contention would usually be wrong. It is utterly implausible, however, to contend that people in nation N have never asked themselves what they are able to do or to be. In that way the Capabilities Approach, by remaining close to the ground, enables us to bypass the confused and confusing abstract debate over rights and imperialism.

More generally, as we ponder the whole issue of pluralism and cultural values, we should bear in mind that no culture is a monolith. All cultures contain a variety of voices, and frequently what passes for "the" tradition of a place is simply the view of the most powerful members of the culture, who have had more access to writing and political expression. Before we could have a decent empirical account of "the" views of a culture, we would need to search out the views of minorities, women, rural people, and other groups whose views are likely to get short shrift in canonical accounts. Once we understand this point, it is very difficult to think of traditional values as having any normative authority at all: tradition gives us only a conversation, a debate, and we have no choice but to evaluate the different positions within it. The Capabilities Approach suggests that we do so using the idea of human dignity for all as our guide.

Nonetheless, we should not ignore the fact that people's choices differ, and that respect for people requires respecting the areas of freedom around them within which they make these choices. Some choices will be personal and idiosyncratic, but many will involve cultural or religious or ethnic or political identities. In framing any normative conception, then, we need to attend carefully to respect for choice and make sure that we protect the spaces within which people express themselves in accordance with their choices. We need to do so all the more clearly and explicitly when our approach makes definite claims about the normative content of political values. We need to be sure that this content does not inappropriately stifle people's capacity for choice in areas of central meaning in their lives. For example, insisting on the mandatory provision of certain forms of life-saving medical treatment, such as blood transfusions, would slight the conscientious choice of Jehovah's Witnesses not to accept transfusions. Problems of this type are avoided by making capability, and not functioning, the appropriate political goal.

Sen, as we have seen, takes a stand on issues of content by focusing attention on education and health, as well as on gender equality. My own, more explicit list, however, makes a more extensive and definite set of commitments, and is thus far more vulnerable to the criticism that it might be too intrusive or biased in the direction of one set of religious or cultural values rather than another. Because I believe that freedom of cultural and religious expression is an important issue, I have integrated a sensitivity to cultural pluralism into my view in several ways.

First, the capabilities list is the outgrowth of a process of critical normative argument, centrally involving the notion of human dignity. Like all respectable philosophical arguments, this one is set forth to be criticized, rebutted, engaged: people can ponder it and, if they find it persuasive, accept it. The list is open-ended and subject to ongoing revision and rethinking.

Second, my approach deliberately specifies the items on the list in a somewhat abstract and general way. This is so precisely to accommodate the specifying and deliberating by citizens, legislatures, and courts that would be required before any such abstract principles could be realized in a constitution or other founding political document with any legitimacy. Within certain parameters it is perfectly appropriate that different nations should do this differently, taking their histories and special circumstances into account. Thus, for example, a free speech right that suits Germany well (allowing anti-Semitic writing and political organizing to be completely banned) would probably be too restrictive in the different climate of the United States (which has held that the idea of freedom of speech under the First Amendment protects such activities). There are different legitimate approaches to defining and protecting the freedom of speech, though some policies are also unacceptably repressive. Whether a situation falls below the threshold of adequacy will typically be determined "on the ground," by confronting a wide range of cases, but we can certainly say that any policy that assigns differing degrees of freedom of speech to different groups of citizens will automatically fall below the threshold.

Third, the list is put forward as part of a free-standing "partial moral conception," to use John Rawls's phrase; that is, it is explicitly introduced for political purposes only, and without any grounding in metaphysical ideas of the sort that divide people along lines of culture and religion. As Rawls says of his basic principles, we can view this list, and the theoretical approach in which it is embedded, as a "module" that can be endorsed by people who have very different conceptions, both religious and secular, of the ultimate meaning and purpose of life. They will link it to their religious or secular comprehensive doctrines in many ways. Like the Universal Declaration of Human Rights, the Capabilities Approach seeks an agreement for practical political purposes and deliberately avoids comment on the deep divisive issues about God, the soul, the limits of human knowledge, and so on, that divide people along lines of doctrine. Such a strategy is a way of expressing respect for diversity, much as a doctrine of non-Establishment, in the area of religion, can be seen as a way of expressing equal respect for all citizens, no matter what their religion or nonreligion. Indeed, in my more detailed work on religion and capability, I strongly defend a non-Establishment doctrine, as well as a very strong Free Exercise doctrine, as essential protectors of human capability and equality in the area of religion.

Fourth, my approach employs a list of capabilities, and the job of government is understood to be that of raising all citizens above the threshold on all ten capabilities. Such a task is explicitly distinguished from the idea of pushing citizens into the associated functionings: people who have a capability have an option, a zone of freedom. They may choose the associated functioning (for example, eating a nutritious diet) or they may avoid it (by fasting or by choosing an unhealthy lifestyle). The focus on capabilities as political goals protects pluralism. Many people who are willing to support a given capability as a fundamental entitlement would feel violated were the associated functioning made basic. Thus the right to vote can be endorsed by believing citizens, such as the Amish, who would feel deeply violated by mandatory voting because it goes against their religious conception. The free exercise of religion can be endorsed by people who would totally object to any establishment of religion that would dragoon all citizens into some type of religious functioning (mandatory religious oaths, religious tests for office, and so forth). Vasanti, a religious person, will use the religious freedom that the constitution of India grants her; if her friend Kokila is nonreligious, she will not use that freedom. Both, however, can endorse that constitutional provision: it is a good idea for all citizens to have such a zone of freedom, they can agree, because religious differences exist in India, and they respect their fellow citizens.

Fifth, the major liberties that protect pluralism are central items on the capabilities list. The freedom of speech, the freedom of association, the freedom of conscience, political access and opportunity—all these are crucial elements of a society that protects cultural and religious pluralism. By placing them on the list we give them a central and non-negotiable place. Contrast a political conception that simply defers to local traditions, whatever these may be: in many, if not most, societies of the world, such a political approach would not protect pluralism, because many local traditions do not endorse the free exercise of religion and the other elements of a meaningful pluralism. Respect for pluralism is in this way totally unlike cultural relativism or deference to tradition: it requires the society to take a stand on some overarching values that protect all citizens in their choices.

Finally, the "colonialism" critique supposes that the framers of such a list will urge governments (particularly powerful Western governments) to charge into nations that do not uphold the values embodied in the approach and impose it by force. The Capabilities Approach, however, utterly repudiates any such way of proceeding. My version insists on a strong separation between issues of justification and issues of implementation. I believe that good arguments can justify this list as a good basis for political principles all around the world. (Even justification involves a democratic element, in the sense that the approach will be justified only if it can be shown to converge, over the long haul, with the deliverances of informed desire.) Justification provides concerned parties with good reasons for promoting the approach in their nations and for working to embody it in international documents. But it is a totally different matter to countenance intervention with the affairs of a state that does not recognize or implement the goals of the approach. If the political approach itself incorporates a strong defense of national sovereignty, as my version of the Capabilities Approach does (arguing that national sovereignty is an important expression of human freedom and of the basic entitlement of all human beings to give themselves laws of their own choosing), then it has already erected a strong barrier against forcible "humanitarian intervention" with the affairs of any state that meets a minimum standard of legitimacy. (I take that to be a much lower standard than that of full justice, which, in all likelihood, no existing state fully meets.)

I hold (following standard accounts of humanitarian intervention) that military and economic sanctions are justified only in certain very grave circumstances involving traditionally recognized crimes against humanity, such as genocide. Even when there are such crimes, it is often a strategic mistake to intervene, particularly if the nation is a democratic one that can be persuaded to repudiate the heinous acts. Thus, although I have argued that the killings of Muslims in the Indian state of Gujarat in 2002 meet the definition of genocide, I also hold that it would have been extremely unwise for any foreign power to intervene in the internal affairs of India, a nation with a thriving democracy. International condemnation of the atrocities is important, as is the refusal to admit the perpetrators as honored guests in one's own nation. (The United States wisely refused a visa to Narendra Modi, the Chief Minister of the State of Gujarat and a major perpetrator of the genocidal assault.) But so long as there is a decent chance that democracy itself can address the issue—as by now, seven years later, it has to a large degree done—it would be totally mistaken to intervene forcibly.

The main worry of the objector, then, seems unjustified. It is difficult to object to recommending something to everyone as a good idea, backed by good arguments, once it becomes clear that state sovereignty, grounded in the consent of the people, is a very important part of the whole package.

6

THE NATION AND GLOBAL JUSTICE

The early versions of the Capabilities Approach focused on the nation state, asking how well nations were doing in promoting the human capabilities of their citizens. The comparative use of the approach in the reports of the United Nations Development Programme is also nation-centered, ranking nations against one another in a variety of ways, but saying nothing, in the rankings, about obligations of richer countries to promote the capabilities of people in poorer nations. (The *Arab Development Report* does, by contrast, focus on supranational regions.) My initial use of the approach to construct a theory of social justice focused, once again, on the nation, suggesting that the task of government, in each nation, is to provide support for the Central Capabilities of all.

The nation is not just a convenient starting place: it has moral importance. Nations—reasonably democratic ones, at any rate—are systems of principles and laws that have their ultimate source in the people. They are thus important expressions of people's autonomy, that is, their entitlement to live under laws of their own choosing. Thus key aspects of the Capabilities Approach, especially its respect for practical reason and for political empowerment, lead it to accord the nation a central standing and to pursue a world in which national sovereignty is protected for reasonably democratic nations. In such a world nations would not (as they risk doing today) lose their power to multinational corporations and global financial networks that have minimal, if any, accountability. Whether the nation is the only entity that has the right sort of accountability to be a vehicle for the expression of autonomy is an empirical question, but until now no larger entity would appear to be accountable enough. Even the European Union (EU) has deficits in this regard.

Nations may be large and diverse, like India, with its 350 languages and 1.2 billion people. They may be federations, like both India and the United States. But they have a unified basic political structure of which the constitution is a key part, and that document, which defines people's basic entitlements, has its source in "We, the people." (This phrase has become standard at the opening of democratic constitutions; for example, it begins the constitutions of the United States, India, and South Africa.) The EU has some of these features, but at present, at least, it does not have enough accountability and responsiveness to satisfy many of its constituents. If it ever moves in that direction, it will probably begin to resemble a federal nation like the United States and India. A world state, were one ever to come into being, would probably be very unsatisfactory from the point of view of human autonomy, because it would be too insensitive to the diverse views of people from different experiences and traditions.

The nation, then, has a moral role that is securely grounded in the Capabilities Approach, because the approach gives central importance to people's freedom and self-definition. And most democratic nations, wisely and efficiently administered, can do pretty well at securing for their people the capabilities on the list. Nonetheless, today's world contains inequalities in basic life chances that seem unconscionable from the standpoint of justice. Just as it seems intolerable that a person's basic opportunities in life should be circumscribed by that person's race or gender or class, so too does it seem insupportable that basic opportunities should be grossly affected by the luck of being born in one nation rather than another. And yet such is the case. Life expectancy, educational and employment opportunities, and health—in short, all the items on the list—vary greatly across national boundaries, and these inequalities are rapidly increasing. Moreover, the influences that generate them are present from the very start of every human life—and even earlier, since maternal nutrition and health care are a major source of unequal life opportunities. If basic justice requires that a person's entitlements not be curtailed by arbitrary features, then justice is ubiquitously violated in the current world order, and the bare existence of the inequality (pushing many people beneath the capability threshold) is reason enough to do something about it.

There are, however, additional reasons to think that richer nations bear responsibility for assisting the efforts of poorer nations. One reason that is important to some, though it is controversial, is that many of the problems of poorer nations were caused by colonial exploitation, which prevented them from industrializing and robbed them of natural resources, among other things. Redistribution in the present seems an appropriate form of remediation for the past.

If we do not accept that backward-looking argument, however, we can still claim that there are features of the current world order that make redistribution mandatory. The world economy is to a large degree controlled by the richer nations and by the corporations that influence their choices. Not surprisingly, they control the system in their own interest. (Adam Smith already noted that corporations, like a "standing army," coerce the political process in ways that are not even wise domestically, but that are most unfair to poorer nations with which the richer have dealings.) The rules of global competition are in many ways advantageous to the richer nations, as are the policies of the World Bank and the International Monetary Fund. These are features of the world right now that make it reasonable to conclude that the poorer nations are not competing on a level playing field. Special attention to their circumstances and redistributive action seem important to right that imbalance.

If we ask ourselves why we, as individuals, should support policies that involve redistribution between nations, we must acknowledge that every day, in countless actions and choices, we form part of that same, allegedly unfair, global economy, affecting lives at a distance. The simplest consumer purchase—for example, that of a soft drink or a pair of jeans—affects lives on the other side of the world. Someone might maintain that inequalities on Mars don't matter to us, have no claim on us, because we have no causal connection with those people and their situation. That argument cannot possibly be made about distant people in today's world. Even were the global economy not unfair to poorer nations, it engages us with them and gives us reasons to think responsibly about how those engagements should continue.

In the case of the nation, the solution to inequalities centrally involves its political structure, its scheme of institutions, and its assignment of duties. If it is correct that a world state would be a bad idea, we cannot rely on an overarching political structure in the same way when we enter the world arena. Therefore it becomes much less clear who has the duties corresponding to the capability entitlements we may think all world citizens have. The presence of entitlements is independent of the existence of a state that bears the duties corresponding to them. But entitlements are correlative with duties, so who has the duties that correspond to the entitlements of world citizens to a decent living standard? Their own nations, in the first place. After that, the governments of richer nations ought to give a minimum of 2 percent of GDP to poorer nations. Multinational corporations, international agencies and agreements, nongovernmental organizations—all these play a part in securing the capabilities of all world citizens. Because our world is fluid and large-scale changes rightly affect the distribution of duties, any assignment of responsibilities should be provisional. Thus the world order will never deliver the level of capability security that we rightly demand from a just nation. But we can do a lot better than we have done so far to foster human capabilities around the world.

Most approaches to global justice in earlier eras were nation-centered in the wrong way. They not only held, correctly, that national sovereignty is an important human good, but they also held, incorrectly, that nations have no obligations to other nations beyond a thin list in the area of war and peace. Both Kant and John Rawls, for example, envisage the search for global principles as taking the form of a *two-stage bargain:* nations first fix their principles internally, and then, at a second stage that cannot call into question any prior agreement (including agreements about economic distribution), the representatives of the nations meet to make a bargain among them. Because this bargain is between nations and not people, and because it cannot alter anything about the nation's internal allocation of duties and opportunities, it is bound to be, and is, quite thin, involving matters of treaty-keeping, war, and peace, but not involving any economic redistribution. If we accept the idea that all people deserve certain core life opportunities as a matter of basic justice, this approach seems woefully inadequate. It is probably inadequate even by its own lights, as I try to show in *Frontiers of Justice*, but making that argument requires patient textual work, which it is unnecessary to replicate here. The use of basically Rawlsian ideas by Thomas Pogge and Charles Beitz to develop the idea of a *global contract* supplies a more promising starting point.

The other prominent approach to global justice that the Capabilities Approach rejects is that of some consequentialist thinkers (most of them utilitarian), who see the problem of global justice as primarily a matter of personal philanthropy. (Peter Unger's utilitarian view is a striking instance of this type.) According to this view, people are obligated to give quite a lot of their wealth and income to assist people in deprived circumstances. It is recommended that they do so by donating to some appropriate transnational charitable organization, such as UNICEF, Oxfam, or CARE. Such approaches have all the problems of utilitarian and consequentialist approaches that we have already discussed. But they have a prior and more glaring problem: they neglect the role of institutions. Suppose a nation attempted to solve its distributional problems through private philanthropy. It doesn't work, and we know that. First, it creates enormous collective-action problems. Nations, when they are just, find ways of assigning to each a fair share of benefits and burdens, but individuals acting on their own will act inefficiently and without coordination. Second, it creates fairness problems: for if needs are really going to be met, then those who pay will have to do more than their fair share to make up for the fact that some shirk their duties. The world version of the personal philanthropic view has both of these problems.

It also has others. Imagine a world in which people really did follow Unger's advice, devoting themselves utterly to maximizing utility (satisfaction) averaged over the entire globe. There would be nothing left of the sense that people have lives that are their own to live, and some discretion about how to do that. Utilitarian morality gobbles up the entire space of a life, a criticism made famous in one form by philosopher Bernard Williams, who argued that utilitarianism cannot make sense of the idea of personal integrity, the importance of the fact that my life and my actions are my own. One nice thing about political structure is that it gives people a clear and finite list of duties and then leaves the rest to them, thus creating a helpful distinction between what I owe to distant others and what I may use for my own purposes (my family, my friends, my pet causes, and so on).

Finally, let's look at the world Unger recommends. It would be run by Oxfam and the other nongovernmental organizations, because if people did what Unger recommends, those organizations would be richer and more powerful than nations. However fine these organizations are—and let's just assume that they are as honest, efficient, and wise as we could wish them to be—still they are not accountable to people in the way that a democratic nation is accountable. If they listen to anyone when setting strategy, it is, most often, to their big donors. We would not like a world in which they (their trustees, their most wealthy donors) had all the power and the agenda-setting opportunity. Ironically—since the view is, in inspiration, egalitarian—such a scenario would mean that a global elite would have much more power than democratically elected governments.

In short, private philanthropy has done some good, and nongovernmental organizations that receive most of their support from private philanthropy have done great good in many cases. Many distinctions must be made, however, as to what forms of private aid are genuinely valuable for people, promoting such crucial values as equal respect and empowerment.

We need, then, an institutional solution to global problems. Working back from the starting point that all world citizens are entitled to support that puts them securely above the threshold on all ten Central Capabilities, we cannot move directly to the assignment of duties to individuals: key duties must be assigned to institutions. Any other sort of solution runs into insuperable practical and conceptual difficulties. A world state, however, is probably a bad idea. It would be unlikely to have the type of accountability we think the government of a state ought to have. The EU is not a good harbinger in this respect, and the United Nations is a positive disaster when it comes to accountability of representatives to the entirety of a people. Even if those problems could be overcome, a world state would probably flatten differences too much. Differences of history and culture have a legitimate bearing on a nation's interpretations of the capability threshold for specific capabilities, and this legitimate diversity can be maintained in a world of nations, but with much more difficulty, if at all, under a world state. Should a nation fall victim to tyranny or state failure, moreover, other nations—as well as subnational and supranational institutions—can respond to requests for aid from its people. A world state could not call in any aid from outside. For all these reasons, then, we should probably not aspire to build a world state.

At this point, workers on the approach will reasonably differ about how the moral duties embodied in the Capabilities Approach should be enforced. Some will defend a robust role for enforceable international agreements in areas such as labor, environment, and human rights. Some will even hold that forcible military and/or economic intervention is justified when a state fails to do justice to basic entitlements in at least some of these areas. My own position, certainly not the only one a proponent of the approach can take, is that national sovereignty is sufficiently important that military intervention is never justified when a nation has a decent minimum of democratic legitimacy; even when that condition is not fulfilled it is generally a very bad idea for prudential reasons. Economic sanctions, too, should be used only in the gravest of cases, for example, that of South Africa under apartheid, where a vast majority of the population was effectively excluded from governance. (Where no state with a claim to even minimal legitimacy exists, the moral argument for nonintervention loses its force, but prudential considerations will still frequently dictate nonintervention.) Persuasion is always appropriate, however, and it is a very good thing if nations can be persuaded to ratify international agreements in major areas of human capability. Once ratified by the nation, they are then binding on the nation and can be enforced by normal domestic mechanisms, as well as by pressure from the community of nations. This position on global governance will seem tepid and thin not only to those who seek a more aggressive international human rights regime but also to those who would prefer to prioritize international agreements in the area of human welfare. I believe my position to be justified by a sound moral argument, but the argument should, and will, continue.

The institutional solution must, then, be thin and decentralized. We have a lot of work to do in assessing how much and what sort of decentralization will be optimal. The institutions involved in solving global problems will prominently include the existing nations, which have duties both to their own people and, in the case of the richer nations, to the poorer nations. A network of international treaties and other agreements can impose some norms on the community of nations, while corporations and nongovernmental organizations can also play a part in promoting human capabilities in the regions in which they operate. Such an allocation should remain tentative and incomplete, responsive to the changing conditions of the world community. (Fifty years ago, the power of multinational corporations would have been difficult to foresee, and any solution that omitted it would need to be altered today.) Clearly, further work on these important issues—as yet undertheorized by the Capabilities Approach—remains of the utmost importance for the future.

7

PHILOSOPHICAL INFLUENCES

The Capabilities Approach is a modern view, but it has a long history. Both Sen and I strongly insist that the intuitive ideas that lie behind it have their roots in many different cultures, and probably in all cultures. Questions about a person's opportunities and options, what she is really in a position to do and to be, are ubiquitous in human life; they are probably part not just of every culture but of every individual life. Moreover, the dissatisfaction and protest to which the approach responds are also ubiquitous. Where do people not say, "I want to do X, but the circumstances of my life don't give me a chance"? To this sort of common discontent, the approach responds by saying, "Yes indeed, in some very important areas you ought to be able to do what you have in mind, and if you aren't able, that is a failure of basic justice." I would go further and say that the connection of human opportunities with ideas of basic entitlement and justice that the approach traces is also ubiquitous. Sen, similarly, has emphasized that the roots of ideas of human entitlement and human rights are present in India and China, as well as in European traditions.

Even at the level of philosophical theory, the Capabilities Approach has many sources. For Sen, the ideas of Rabindranath Tagore and Mahatma Gandhi—not to mention a wide range of earlier Indian rationalist thinkers—were at least as formative as the Western sources I shall describe here. This chapter is therefore deliberately incomplete, reflecting the fact that Sen has written extensively about the Indian sources of his ideas and that mere summary of his writings on this point would not be very useful. My own account of women's freedom and capability has also been influenced by Tagore's humanist philosophical and literary writings. We should bear in mind, too, that some of the European sources were themselves in conversation with the Indian sources on which Sen draws. (Tagore and Mill are intellectual first cousins, for example, in that both owe a large debt to Auguste Comte.) Currently, theoretical work on the Capabilities Approach is being carried on enthusiastically by scholars from many different nations and traditions, prominently including people from non–Euro-American traditions; this work shows that the approach has broad appeal and support.

Among Euro-American antecedents, the most important sources of my version of the Capabilities Approach are works from ancient Greece and Rome, although Smith, Kant, Mill, and Marx have also greatly influenced my formulations. John Rawls's work has been of the utmost importance, particularly in convincing me that the view ought to be expressed as a type of political liberalism. T. H. Green and Ernest Barker were not known to me when I developed the view, but the discovery of similarities of approach has been illuminating.

These Western traditions also figure among Sen's intellectual antecedents, which include humanist Marxism, John Stuart Mill's views of liberty and self-development, and, particularly, Adam Smith's writings on both the economy and the moral sentiments. Because Smith was a primary source of the modern reformulation and reinvigoration of Aristotelian and Stoic ideas, Sen's lifelong interest in Smith connects him to those earlier texts. Ernest Barker, moreover, was such a towering figure at Cambridge, shaping generations of scholars, that it would not be surprising if his neo-Aristotelian influence reached Sen in his youth.

This excursus into intellectual history is not part of the justification of the approach, which can stand on its own. It does, however, help show that ideas of this sort have a wide-ranging resonance and appeal; and this, in turn, may help establish that they can become the object of an overlapping consensus in a society containing many comprehensive views of value.

Aristotle and the Stoics

In one way, the earliest Western source for the Capabilities Approach is Socrates, who emphasized the importance of critical thinking through dialogue with others. Socrates, however, had no developed political theory. The earliest and most important Western historical source for the Capabilities Approach is, then, the political and ethical thought of Aristotle. Aristotle believed that political planners need to understand what human beings require for a flourishing life. He explicitly said that his ethical writings about the flourishing human life were intended as guides for his society's future politicians, so that they could see what it was they were trying to achieve.

Because choice was all-important for Aristotle—no action counts as virtuous in any way unless it is mediated by the person's own thought and selection—he did not instruct politicians to make everyone perform desirable activities. Instead, they were to aim at producing capabilities or opportunities. Aristotle was no liberal, but he did think that satisfaction achieved without choice is unworthy of the dignity of human beings. And he understood that, even where no prohibitions exist, impediments to meaningful choice might be supplied by lack of education or conditions of labor that make it impossible to inform oneself or reflect. Aristotle claimed that political planning should focus "above all" on the education of the young, since the neglect of education does great harm to political life. Repeatedly in his writings he identified different levels of human capability (or *dunamis*), roughly corresponding to the distinctions I have introduced (innate capabilities, developed internal capabilities, and, finally, combined capabilities).

Aristotle was particularly adamant that the pursuit of wealth is not an appropriate overall goal for a decent society. Wealth is but a means, and the human values that should guide political planning would be utterly debased and deformed were wealth to be understood as an end in itself. Nor did he favor any account of the overall end of political planning that posited some single homogeneous goal varying only in quantity. In the multifaceted revival of Aristotelian thought that has considerable influence in contemporary moral philosophy, this issue of noncommensurability, so important in the Capabilities Approach, is rightly salient.

Although utilitarianism as such was unknown to him, Aristotle was aware of hedonist views of the good human life that identified the good with the greatest net balance of pleasure over pain, and he made a range of arguments against hedonism that are good arguments today against Benthamite forms of utilitarianism. (With Mill, he held that pleasures differ in quality as well as quantity; he also argued that some pleasures are bad and should not count at all in favor of a project, while some choiceworthy human activities, such as risking one's life for one's country, are not pleasant; there are others, such as seeing, remembering, and knowing, that we would choose even if they brought no pleasure.) In general, he held that pleasure and the satisfaction of desire are utterly unreliable as guides to what is to be promoted in society, since people learn to derive pleasure from all sorts of things, good and bad, depending on the type of education they have had.

Any decent political plan, then, would seek to promote a range of diverse and incommensurable goods, involving the unfolding and development of distinct human abilities. Moreover, it must seek to promote them not just for some overall aggregate but for each and every citizen ("each and every one," Aristotle once said, contrasting this goal with Plato's corporatist idea). Aware of Plato's state, where an overall good condition of society was (allegedly) promoted in ways that permanently subordinated one class of citizens, Aristotle rejected the idea of corporate flourishing as confused: "A city is by nature a plurality . . . The good of each is what preserves each."

Many political thinkers in the much later liberal tradition have had similar insights. What makes Aristotle of continuing centrality for political thought is the way in which he coupled an understanding of choice and its importance with an understanding of human vulnerability. A great biologist and the son of a doctor, Aristotle was never tempted to view the human being as a disembodied creature. He upbraided his students for viewing with disgust the animal body and the messy stuffs from which it is made. He understood that a human being is a kind of animal, and that all animals move from birth through infancy and childhood to maturity and then, if they live on, to old age, with its many infirmities. (He devoted an entire treatise to the topic of old age, another to the topic of sleep, another to memory and failures of memory.)

Because Aristotle understood human vulnerability, he saw that government needed to address issues such as the purity of a water supply and the quality of air, as well as education. Vulnerability cannot be removed altogether, of course, but Aristotle did lay emphasis on the way in which some cities supported human weakness better than others. He proposed that government provide nutrition, in the form of communal meals that promote fellowship and friendship as well as health. Richer people would pay for the costs of their own meals, but the participation of poor people would be supported by the city. Under such a scheme, fully half of the city's land would be publicly owned, and the produce from it would subsidize both public meals and civic festivals (such as the festivals at which tragedies were performed in his day); even land that is privately owned would be available for use by people in need. These are some of the consequences Aristotle derived from his idea that the job of government is to make all citizens capable of leading a flourishing life in accordance with their choice.

Aristotle's philosophical thought has some grave limitations. Although his ideal city is democratic in the sense that citizens should take turns ruling and being ruled, he defined the participant group much too narrowly. He was happy with a system like that of the Athens of his day, in which only free adult nonimmigrant males were citizens and in which slavery was practiced. And he would favor even more exclusions than Athens practiced: manual laborers, farmers, and sailors were to be excluded from citizenship in his ideal city. He seemed to lack the basic idea of human equality, of a worth all humans share across differences of gender, class, and ethnicity. Nor did he even ask about obligations we might have to support the lives of people outside our own borders. Like all ancient Greek thinkers, he showed no sensitivity to the thought that people have different comprehensive views of how to live and that government ought to respect them by giving them space for such choices. He assumed that the right way to proceed is to identify the best account of flourishing and then to make people capable of flourishing according to that account.

Stoicism remedied the first and second of these deficiencies, though not the third. The most influential school of ethical and political thought in Greco-Roman antiquity, and perhaps the most influential philosophical school at any time in the Western tradition, it exercised such a widespread sway, particularly in Rome, that every educated person, and many who were not educated, were at some level guided by it. Even when Christianity replaced Stoicism as the daily creed of the Roman Empire, it was a Christianity profoundly influenced by Stoicism, and the whole history of subsequent Western thought in the European Christian tradition bears the impress of Stoic philosophical ideas. (The idea of "natural law," one primary source of the modern human rights movement, is primarily a Stoic idea. Medieval Aristotelian thinkers developed it, but early modern Protestant thinkers such as Grotius and Kant read the Stoic authors directly, deriving ideas about international duties and entitlements from that source.)

The Stoics taught that every single human being, just by virtue of being human, has dignity and is worthy of reverence. Our ability to perceive ethical distinctions and to make ethical judgments was held to be the "god within," and as such is worthy of boundless reverence. Ethical capacity is found in all human beings, male and female, slave and free, high-born and low-born, rich and poor. Wherever we find this basic human capacity, then, we ought to respect it, and that respect should be equal; we should treat the artificial distinctions created by society as trivial and insignificant. This idea of equal respect for humanity lies at the heart of "natural law," the moral law that ought to guide us, even when we are outside the realm of positive law. (Later on, Christian ideas of human equality, themselves strongly influenced by Stoicism, joined with the Stoic ideas to strengthen notions of equal human entitlement.)

More than most, the Stoics put their views into practice: they campaigned for the equal education of women, and their ranks included one former slave (Epictetus), one foreigner from the far reaches of the empire (Seneca, born in Spain), and various women (whose writings, unfortunately, do not survive), not to mention the "new man" Cicero, whose nonaristocratic origins are a constant theme in his writings. Because their thinking was not bounded by the walls of the city-state, they developed elaborate doctrines of duties to humanity, including proper conduct during wartime. These ideas had a formative influence on modern founders of international law such as Grotius, Pufendorf, and Kant.

The idea of human dignity, and of its boundless and equal worth, is the primary contribution of Stoicism to the Capabilities Approach. What political principles and actions did this idea suggest? Cicero and the Stoics held that human dignity should never be abused by making it subject to the arbitrary will of another. Because human beings have dignity, are not mere objects, it is bad to treat them like objects, pushing them around without their consent. And because human dignity is equal, it is abhorrent to set up ranks and orders of human beings, allowing some to tyrannize others.

The Romans themselves derived a range of different political lessons from these ideas. Cicero, passionate defender of the Roman republic in its waning days, believed that human dignity requires republican institutions through which people could govern themselves without arbitrary tyranny. He defended the assassination of Julius Caesar in those terms, and he risked (and ultimately lost) his life in defense of the republic. (Cicero's insights are incorporated in the Capabilities Approach, in many ways.) Other leading Romans fully agreed with Cicero about the republic, whether they were Stoics or not, and two anti-imperial movements during the early years of the empire had Stoic roots. Some Romans, however, believed that only monarchy could put an end to the tumult of civil war. Some later Roman Stoics thought, or at least said—since freedom of speech was compromised under the empire—that a decently accountable monarchy might be acceptable. One, Marcus Aurelius, agreed to be adopted and to become, himself, the emperor. The experience of empire showed, however, that Cicero was correct: once a monarchy is in place, nothing prevents it from turning in an arbitrary and oppressive direction. So as time went on, it came to seem more and more reasonable for Stoic thought to ally itself firmly with the idea of accountable republican institutions: only within these can human beings live lives worthy of human dignity.

Stoicism also contained, however, the seeds of a more quietistic response, suggested by its anti-Aristotelian ideas about human invulnerability. Because the Stoics taught that dignity was all-important and material conditions utterly unimportant, it was possible to maintain that the soul was always free within, whether or not institutions enslaved it on the outside. In one striking example of this general point, Seneca's famous letter on slavery asks masters to show respect to their slaves and to treat them like full-fledged and equal human beings; but it does not attack the institution of slavery, which Seneca holds to be compatible with a dignified free life within. These disturbing conclusions were reached not by compromising the Stoic commitment to equal worth but, instead, by denying the Aristotelian thought of human vulnerability: external conditions are not really important to a person's attempt to live well, so it isn't necessary for law and government to supply those conditions.

The Seventeenth and Eighteenth Centuries: Natural Law, Human Vulnerability

Typically, thought about "natural law" in the seventeenth and eighteenth centuries—and thus the core of the classical education given to people bound for politics and government—melded Aristotelian with Stoic elements. Although different combinations of ideas could be made, one attractive and enduring marriage, compatible with mainstream Christian beliefs, was that between Stoic ideas of the equal worth of all human beings and Aristotelian ideas about human vulnerability. Despite the enduring attraction of Stoic ideas of the soul's invulnerability, Aristotle's view was strongly commended by common sense and by most people's experience of loss, age, the damages of war, and so forth. Hugo Grotius, Adam Smith, Kant, and the American founders all accepted the Stoic idea of equal dignity, while turning to Aristotle to understand the many ways in which human beings need help from the world in order to live well.

One particularly interesting use of the mixed view was made by Roger Williams, a British classical scholar trained in the Stoic natural-law tradition, who moved to America and founded the colony of Rhode Island, the first in which genuine religious liberty obtained. His eloquent philosophical writings on liberty of conscience described conscience as a source of equal dignity in all human beings (thus following the Stoics), but they insisted, as well, that worldly conditions are crucial if conscience is to unfold itself without deformation or suppression (thus following Aristotle). The capacity for free religious searching is among the Central Capabilities; Williams's writings and political practice help us see what governmental support for that capability ought to look like.

The eighteenth century saw a widespread fascination with Stoic ideas of equal dignity. These ideas influenced republican thinkers on both sides of the Atlantic, who understood the primary task of republicanism, in Stoic terms, as that of preventing domination and hierarchy. Most often, however, these ideas were borrowed in combination with an Aristotelian understanding of human vulnerability. The task of government thus came to be understood as that of protecting certain core human abilities so that they might develop and become effective. For our purposes, however, two key texts will suffice, significant in their own right and also highly influential in the American Founding. The first is Adam Smith's book *The Wealth of Nations*, a work that profoundly influenced both European thought (Kant, for example) and the American Founding.

Smith's writings are suffused with Stoicism, and he wrote to an audience that he expected to be steeped in Stoic ideas as well. Since he rejected the Stoic doctrine of invulnerability, however, he turned to Aristotle for a correct understanding of the worth of family, friends, and many of the material conditions of human flourishing.

Some of the impediments to human capabilities that Smith saw in the England of his time consisted in wrong-headed and intrusive legal restrictions, such as restrictions on trade and the free movement of labor. In such cases Smith urged deregulation, and he has thus become a favorite source for libertarians. It is clear, however, that such a reading of Smith is inadequate. His touchstone was always the question, What form of action by government permits human abilities to develop and human equality to be respected? When government action seemed to him to inhibit the development of human capabilities, he was for less of it—but of course he understood quite well that it would take law to unmake law. Thus he supported the abolition of apprenticeship and the introduction of laws against monopolies and restrictions on lobbying by powerful finan-

cial interests, which, in his view, make citizens' influence on the political process grossly unequal, guaranteeing that government will
be held hostage to what he called a "standing army" of wealthy
elites. He also favored the abolition of the slave trade, and indeed he
campaigned on behalf of this cause. He showed at least some sympathy with wage regulations that favor workmen. He was especially
concerned that all workmen should be guaranteed the "lowest rate
that is consistent with common humanity," which means, as he saw
it, an income sufficient to maintain a household with a wife and
enough children to guarantee that two survive to adulthood. These
proposals are supported by considerations of justice as well as ef-
ficiency. Smith's concern for equal respect also extended outside
national boundaries: he strenuously opposed colonization on the
grounds that it is a way of exploiting the colonized people, who lose
both political autonomy and economic control.

Among Smith's most radical defense of government intervention
is a set of arguments late in *The Wealth of Nations* calling for government provision of free compulsory public education—which, at the
time of his writing, was in place in Scotland but utterly neglected in
England. The context of the discussion is a set of Aristotelian obser-
vations concerning the waste of human abilities among the working classes. Early in the work, Smith emphasized the fact that habit
and education play a profound role in shaping human abilities: the
philosopher and the street porter differ in education, not by nature,
although the "vanity" of the former supposes otherwise. Much of
The Wealth of Nations is accordingly dedicated to documenting the
many factors that can cause key human abilities to fail to develop.
Some of these factors are straightforwardly physical. Poverty is un-
favorable to life and health. Some nations are so poor that they are
forced to practice infanticide and to leave the elderly and sick to be

devoured by wild beasts. Even in Britain, Smith insisted, high child mortality was characteristic of the working, and not the more prosperous, classes. He noted that "poverty, though it does not prevent the generation, is extremely unfavourable to the rearing of children. The tender plant is produced, but in so cold a soil and so severe a climate, soon withers and dies." Elsewhere, Smith generalized the point: any class that cannot support itself from wages will be afflicted with "want, famine, and mortality."

These passages show Smith breaking with the Stoics and developing an Aristotelian account of the human being and of basic needs. He reminded his reader that human dignity is not something rockhard. It is, rather, a "tender plant" that will wither if it encounters a cold soil and a severe climate. This means that we cannot take the view that the distribution of material goods is irrelevant to human dignity: for dignity requires, at the very least, life, and the lives of children are in the hands of these material arrangements.

But it is in his lengthy discussion of education that Smith developed most fully his ideas about the fragility of human dignity. The question he faced is whether the state ought to take responsibility for the education of its people and, if so, in what way. He now observed that the newly fashionable division of labor, combined with a lack of general education, has a very pernicious effect on human abilities:

> The man whose whole life is spent in performing a few
> simple operations, of which the effects too are, perhaps,
> always the same, or very nearly the same, has no occasion
> to exert his understanding ... He naturally loses, there-
> fore, the habit of such exertion, and generally becomes as
> stupid and ignorant as it is possible for a human creature

to become . . . Of the great and extensive interests of his
country, he is altogether incapable of judging; and unless
very particular pains have been taken to render him otherwise, he is equally incapable of defending his country in
war . . . But in every improved and civilized society this is
the state into which the labouring poor, that is, the great
body of the people, must necessarily fall, unless government takes some pains to prevent it.

The danger, Smith continued, is not great when we are dealing
with people who are not desperately poor, for even if their children
will eventually perform a monotonous job, they typically do so only
after receiving a primary education. Moreover, the relatively comfortable usually do not work as many hours as the poor do, so they
can keep some part of their day to "perfect themselves" in some
branch of knowledge or activity other than that of their trade. The
public sphere, therefore, does not need to worry much about their
loss of human capacities.

It is otherwise with the common people. They have little time to
spare for education. Their parents can scarcely afford to maintain
them even in infancy. As soon as they are able to work, they must
apply to some trade by which they can earn their subsistence. That
trade, too, is generally so simple and uniform as to give little exercise to the understanding; while, at the same time, their labor is
both so constant and so severe that it leaves them little leisure and
less inclination to apply themselves to or even to think of anything
else.

Without education, a person "is as much mutilated and deformed
in his mind, as another is in his body, who is either deprived of some
of its most essential members, or has lost the use of them." Even if

educating the common people does not lead to the nation's overall enrichment, "it would still deserve its attention that they should not be altogether uninstructed."

Smith now argued that the bad situation is not inevitable. No state, he believed, can guarantee all citizens as extensive an education as the rich currently receive at their parents' expense. But it can, like Scotland, provide all with "the most essential parts of education," by requiring them to learn reading, writing, and accounting before they are permitted to take on paid employment. He went on to describe a scheme for low-cost compulsory education in parish schools, in which frivolous subjects such as Latin would be left out, and useful subjects, such as geometry and mechanics, would be put in their place.

Smith attained an insight that lies at the heart of the Capabilities Approach: an understanding that human abilities come into the world in a nascent or undeveloped form and require support from the environment—including support for physical health and especially, here, for mental development—if they are to mature in a way that is worthy of human dignity.

Like Adam Smith's anticipated audience in Britain, Americans in the mid-eighteenth century were steeped in the texts of ancient Greek, and especially Roman, philosophy (besides being steeped in Smith's own works). They focused on the idea of equal human dignity and equal entitlement rather than on the unpromising Stoic idea of human invulnerability. They understood all too well that government could block human capabilities, because they had experienced the hand of tyranny. They also understood that a full set of human capabilities could not be secured in a vacuum: government had a job to do. As the U.S. Declaration of Independence states this ubiquitous idea: "We hold these truths to be self-evident, that all men are created equal, that they are endowed by their Creator with certain unalienable Rights, that among these are Life, Liberty and the pursuit of Happiness.—That to secure these rights, Governments are instituted among Men, deriving their just powers from the consent of the governed." And of course the document goes on to argue that any government that does not deliver on that task may be altered or abolished. Moreover, one of the Declaration's central complaints against George III was his *inaction:* "He has refused his Assent to Laws, the most wholesome and necessary for the public good."

Thus the idea that the American Framers were libertarians, or fans of "negative liberty," is extremely misleading. Like Smith, they knew what they did not like: tyrannical government, bilking the people for the support of selfish elites, while neglecting the welfare of the people. But a dislike of bad government was not a dislike of government per se. To see how the combination of Stoic equality with Aristotelian need worked its way into the Framers' conception of government, let us look more closely at a chapter from a book by one of the period's most influential thinkers, Thomas Paine's *Rights of Man.*

Like other intellectuals at the time of the Founding, Paine disliked a lot of the government action that he saw: monarchical and aristocratic governments in Europe typically exploited the common people for the benefit of the few. The foundation of government, Paine said, is the natural rights of human beings; the proper goal of government is "the good of all, as well individually as collectively." Existing governments, however, did not pursue this goal. Instead, they operated "to create and encrease wretchedness" in the poorer parts of society. In the long chapter entitled "Ways and Means of Improving the Condition of Europe," Paine argued for a complete overhaul both of government action and of taxation. Taxation would cease to be regressive and become progressive. The poor rates would be entirely abolished, and the power of elites to divert taxes away from themselves would be curtailed. (Paine mordantly described "what is called the crown" as "a nominal office of a million sterling a year, the business of which consists in receiving the money.") He proposed a detailed scheme of progressive taxation, starting at a rate of threepence per pound and ascending, in rather short order, for income that exceeded a given level, to a rate of twenty shillings per pound, or 100 percent! (Paine was way ahead of Sweden at its most draconian.)

The revenue thus gained would be used to support human capabilities, in three areas above all: youth, age, and unemployment. Like Smith, Paine favored state-supplied compulsory primary education: "A nation under a well-regulated government should permit none to remain uninstructed. It is monarchical and aristocratical government only that requires ignorance for its support." He noted that young people often took to crime because they had never had an education that would open employment opportunities for them, and he concluded that government inaction was to blame: "When, in countries that are called civilized, we see age going to the workhouse and youth to the gallows, something must be wrong in the system of government." "Civil government," he continued, "does not exist in executions; but in making such provision for the instruction of youth and the support of age, as to exclude, as much as possible, profligacy from the one and despair from the other. Instead of this, the resources of a country are lavished upon kings, upon courts, upon hirelings, impostors, and prostitutes." Calculating that a large proportion of England's poor were either children or people over the age of fifty, he proposed a cash subsidy to poor families, out of surplus tax revenue, of four pounds per year, on condition that the children attend school. He noted that in this way "the poverty of the parents will be relieved, ignorance will be banished from the rising generation, and the number of the poor will hereafter become less, because their abilities, by the aid of education, will be greater." They would thus have employment opportunities that were at present closed to them. For families somewhat less poor, Paine proposed a per-child school subsidy, including money for school supplies. He recommended generous cash subsidies for people over the age of sixty. "This support," he repeatedly stressed, "is not of the nature of a charity but of a right." It was part of the general task of government to support the life-cycle of citizens. To this Paine added an intriguing proposal for public works projects to relieve unemployment. He wanted a lot more government in the area of support for basic human welfare, and a lot less government in the area of elite self-enrichment.

Studying this history we learn that the basic ideas of the Capabilities Approach, including the importance of government support for basic human welfare, are no recent invention; nor are they associated only with European-style social democracy. They are a deep part of mainstream liberal enlightenment thought, in both Europe and North America. This point is peripheral to the primary justification of the approach, since one should not argue from philosophical authority. We may, however, learn how to reply to the charges (frequently made) that the Capabilities Approach is only for non-Western and developing countries, or the charge that it is foreign to American traditions. More important, we may gain confidence in our own proposals when we notice how, operating relatively independent of one another (relatively, since at least some of the American Founders, especially James Madison, knew the works of Smith), people in different parts of the world have reinvented similar ideas as proffered solutions to standing human problems, and we may derive insight from the detail of these historical solutions.

The Nineteenth and Twentieth Centuries: Capabilities against Utilitarianism and Libertarianism

Far from being an approach suited only to pre-industrial societies, the Capabilities Approach has seen some of its most striking political applications in the modern era, where industrial development has given rise to new threats to the capabilities of both children (sent to labor in factories from an early age) and adults (laboring under unsafe and burdensome conditions, without the leverage to contract for a better arrangement). At the same time, the modern era has seen a new awareness of the obstacles to human development imposed by traditional discrimination on the basis of race, sex, and disability, all of which have proven focal points for recent capabilities analysis.

Nineteenth-century Britain saw some striking and influential anticipations of contemporary American discussions about human capability: first, in the writings of John Stuart Mill (1806–1873), which clarified the relationship of political liberty to human self-development and demonstrated the harm done by discrimination to the opportunities and capacities of women. (Mill compared the restrictions imposed by the discriminatory legal regime governing marriage to slavery. As a member of Parliament, he introduced the first bill for women's suffrage.) Mill's influence on American ideas of freedom has been large; his ideas on gender, neglected in Britain in his lifetime, have been formative for women's movements in many nations.

Shortly after Mill's death, an even more extensive use of ideas of human capability was made by T. H. Green (1836–1882), a professor of philosophy who advised the British Liberal party. Green used Aristotelian ideas to repudiate both utilitarianism and libertarianism (which by then had achieved considerable political influence), arguing that the right way to protect human freedom was to create conditions in which people of all sorts were able to make a wide range of choices with sufficient protection from society. Green influentially supported legislation for free compulsory public education, workplace safety regulations, a limitation on working hours, a ban on child labor, and limitations on the type of contract that landlords might make with tenant farmers. These limitations on the freedom of contract, Green argued, could be defended by appeal to "that general freedom of [society's] members to make the best of themselves, which it is the object of civil society to secure." He supported the equal education of women, though he lagged behind Mill in not supporting the franchise. Although Green died young, his work was carried on by his long-lived disciple Ernest Barker (1874–1960), who, a professor for many years at Cambridge University, sowed the seeds of Green's approach in many nations, since at that time Cambridge was a central place of choice for graduate students from many nations. Barker was a distinguished scholar of ancient Greek thought as well as a contemporary theorist, and he made the Aristotelian pedigree of his ideas very clear. In the United States, as in Britain, such ideas were forwarded through legislation protecting workers' rights, establishing compulsory education, fostering the education of poor children, and, ultimately, protecting vulnerable minorities from discrimination—above all during the New Deal and the "Great Society" era.

8

CAPABILITIES AND CONTEMPORARY ISSUES

The Capabilities Approach suggests distinctive methods for dealing with a number of problems currently being faced by social and political theory. Cutting-edge work is being done by capabilities theory in a variety of areas. Descriptions must remain superficial, but they show that the approach promises a new, and relatively unified, perspective on problems that are often treated in isolation from one another. The list is to some extent arbitrary: other issues could easily be added. (Three that come immediately to mind are migration, the Internet, and global warming.)

Disadvantage

A longstanding debate within development economics concerns the right way to think about poverty and disadvantage. Sen has long argued that poverty is best understood as capability failure, not just as shortage of commodities or even of income and wealth. Poverty involves heterogeneous failures of opportunity, which are not always well correlated with income; moreover, people in positions of social exclusion may have difficulty converting income into actual functioning, so income is not even a good proxy for capabilities. In general, income is a means to an end, and capabilities are the end.

One particular difficulty with measuring poverty through income is that available income measures pertain to the household; a focus on income therefore encourages the neglect of sex bias in nutrition, health care, and other aspects of poverty. Looking at poverty in terms of capability failure, by contrast, encourages a focus on how each person is doing and spotlights distributional inequalities in the family. The Capability Approach has also been assertive in demanding that income accounts take cognizance of the value of unpaid domestic work, another key issue in assessing relative disadvantage.

Sen's work on capability failure grew out of his Nobel Prize–winning work on famines, in which he emphasized that famine is not caused simply by shortage of food but is a matter of lacking opportunities to obtain the things one needs (because of unemployment, for example). Its remedy therefore cannot lie simply in food relief or handouts. A genuine solution would require addressing the capability failures of the vulnerable populations, by providing employment and other sources of entitlement to vital commodities. This general point has become a part of uncontroversial mainstream analysis.

The further step of thinking about disadvantage more generally in terms of capability failure, though a natural next move, has not always been taken, partly because the attraction of models that aggregate across elements of lives remains strong, as does the attraction of using income and wealth as proxies for the different life-opportunities that people may or may not have. In *Disadvantage,* Jonathan Wolff and Avner De-Shalit argue vigorously against reducing all the elements of lives to a single numerical scale. They show that any approach that aggregates across the diverse elements of lives is bound to miss things of vital importance when one is attempting to describe the situation of disadvantaged groups and to propose strategies to improve their situation. Disadvantage, they argue, is irreducibly plural, and its different aspects vary to a significant extent independent of one another and of income and wealth. This argument is in the spirit of Sen's views, but it is more detailed and elaborate, and therefore may convince people who have not been persuaded by Sen. Wolff and De-Shalit also show in further detail why income and wealth are not good proxies for relative disadvantage.

In connection with this general analysis of disadvantage, Wolff and De-Shalit extend the approach in two ways. First, they propose a focus not simply on the presence or absence of key capabilities but on their *security*. People need to have not just a capability today but a secure expectation that it will be there tomorrow. One salient aspect of disadvantage is that, even when a group may have access to a capability (employment opportunities, for example), that access is very insecure. Second, although Wolff and De-Shalit remain committed to the separate importance of each capability, they recommend a study of how disadvantages cluster, with one disadvantage leading to another *(corrosive disadvantages)*, and, correspondingly, of how specific capabilities may be particularly fertile in opening up others.

The fertility of a given capability, and the corrosiveness of a given capability failure, are empirical questions whose answers are likely to vary with time and place and with the particular problems of the disadvantaged group. Usually, however, the variation means only that some women, for example, already have capability security with respect to the fertile capability, not that it is not fertile. For Vasanti and for many poor women, access to credit is particularly fertile, opening access to employment, bodily integrity, and political participation. We might think that credit is not so important for women with a fuller educational background and a history of formal employment, who may have fewer worries on that score; but actually, credit is a major issue for many women, particularly at the end of a marriage in which the wife has not had market employment. We can be sure that domestic violence is corrosive all over the world, and that few if any women enjoy full capability security in this regard. Wolff and De-Shalit find that affiliation—having supportive and mutually respectful relationships—is particularly fertile in both of their countries, and we can predict that this is likely to be true elsewhere: isolation makes it much harder to achieve anything.

Gender

In the work of Sen and Nussbaum, the Capabilities Approach has focused on the inequality of women. (Seeds of this emphasis can be found in some historical predecessors, such as the Stoics, Smith, Mill, and Green.) There are two distinct reasons for this emphasis. First, these problems are of huge intrinsic importance. Women are unequal in many respects all over the world, and this is an enormous problem of justice. It is also a development problem, because denial of opportunity to women holds back the productivity of many nations.

Second, these problems are a theoretical litmus test, illustrating vividly why standard development approaches (the GNP approach, utilitarian approaches) are inadequate, and why the Capabilities Approach does better. On the side of philosophy, looking at these problems shows some shortcomings of parts of the classical liberal tradition, which has often conceived of the family as part of a "private sphere" off-limits to social justice. (As John Stuart Mill pointed out, this move was an inconsistency within classical liberalism, not its natural outgrowth, since liberalism at its core is committed to equal liberty and opportunity for all. Leaving the family uncriticized was leaving a little piece of feudal hierarchy uncriticized, and liberalism is rightly subversive of all hierarchies based on birth or status.)

My book *Women and Human Development* shows in detail how alternative approaches in the development sphere, particularly utilitarianism, and even sophisticated informed-desire theories, prove inadequate in confronting the inequality of women. It also addresses the obstacles to women's equality caused by uncritical adherence to tradition. Religions are not always retrograde; when they are, it is usually in alliance with longstanding cultural traditions. Nonetheless, because religion is a sphere of life that deserves state protection and concern, it is often the source of difficult dilemmas, as certain religious demands may run afoul of the demands of sex equality. The book makes a theoretical proposal for the resolution of such dilemmas—arguing (as in *Liberty of Conscience*) that ample space be given for religious free exercise and even for religiously grounded "accommodation," but that the protection of the Central Capabilities always be regarded as a "compelling state interest" that would justify the imposition of a burden on the free exercise of religion. The Indian constitution utterly forbids the practice of "untouchability," a central aspect of traditional Hindu religion. This may be a burden to some, but that burden, as Gandhi argued, is amply justified by the state interest in eradicating discrimination. Similarly in the United States, Bob Jones University lost its tax-exempt status for forbidding interracial dating. The U.S. Supreme Court argued that the compelling state interest of eradicating racism justified the imposition of a financial burden on this evangelical group.

Similar dilemmas are confronted in the area of family privacy. Even if we deny that there is any sphere of human life that is "private" in the sense of being immune to legal regulation, we should also grant that free human lives need spaces for the protection of intimate association and for parental decision-making with regard to children. Some issues are, or should be, easy: we should all agree that domestic violence and child sexual abuse should be aggressively policed by the state. We can grant that child marriage should be illegal and that marital consent should be carefully protected. We can also grant that compulsory primary and secondary education are important ways in which the state limits parents' autonomy (for example, the choice to use a child for wage labor). We can also probably agree that education should teach girls a wide range of skills, giving them exit options from traditional roles, and that their full equality as citizens should be firmly conveyed to them, along with the skills necessary for effective political activity. Other areas of freedom are more difficult: how far to give parents latitude to choose homeschooling, for example, which may not fully convey the message of equality. In India, government support for women's organizations that challenge traditional roles and convey a message of autonomy and equality seems amply justified by the political importance of the capabilities of practical reason and affiliation (both friendship and political participation).

My ongoing work on sexual orientation is strongly linked to the idea of human capabilities, particularly in thinking about the ways in which discrimination on the basis of sexual orientation expresses stigma and reinforces a view that some people are not fully equal.

Thinking about sexual orientation through the lens of the whole list of capabilities makes us seek policies that are not just formally fair, treating similar people similarly, but that go deeper, seeking out the roots of hierarchy and stigma and refusing to approve of arrangements that confer government approval on those sources of inequality. Laws against miscegenation appeared to some to be formally fair, because they treated both races similarly: blacks couldn't marry whites, and whites couldn't marry blacks. But the U.S. Supreme Court understood that such laws convey a message of stigma and inferiority. So, too, do laws forbidding same-sex marriage. These laws are sometimes defended as legitimate exercises of state power to regulate marriage—in much the way that states once defended their antimiscegenation laws. They are, however, unfair in a very similar way, conferring a message of stigma and inferiority. Nor does the remedy of civil unions go far enough. If states had offered "transracial unions" as a separate legal category but continued to deny marriage to interracial couples, we can see that, far from ending stigma and hierarchy, such an arrangement would have reinforced it.

Disability, Aging, and the Importance of Care

An urgent problem of justice that is only now beginning to be confronted by modern societies is how to promote the capabilities of people with a wide range of physical and mental disabilities. Including such people on a basis of equal respect requires not only practical change but theoretical change as well. Just as the full inclusion of women as subjects of political justice required asking questions (about justice inside the family) that had not been asked before, so doing justice to the claims of people with disabilities requires calling into question a very fundamental idea of classical liberalism, namely, that the goal and *raison d'être* of social cooperation is mutual advantage, where advantage is understood in narrow economic terms. The whole idea of the social contract involves such a fiction, and for this reason theories in the social contract tradition had to postpone the problem of disability to a later point in the theoretical structure, after society's basic institutions had already been designed. People with disabilities are, however, equals who need to be taken into account from the beginning in designing any scheme of social cooperation. It is a long and intricate matter to show that theories in the social contract tradition cannot answer this challenge by some minor modification, and that task, which forms the primary substance of *Frontiers of Justice*, cannot be adequately summarized here. Suffice it to say that the task of fully including people with disabilities and supporting their human capabilities requires a new account of social cooperation and the human motives for it, an account focused on benevolence and altruism, not just mutual advantage.

Now of course most theorists in the classical social contract tradition did not believe that people were primarily selfish. (Thomas Hobbes and his modern follower David Gauthier do believe this, but they are atypical.) The reason for assuming that mutual advantage is the goal of the parties to the contract is a reason of parsimony: if a just society can be generated out of weak assumptions (in other words, assuming not altruism or virtue but much less than that), that is itself interesting, and one should always choose the weakest premises from which one's conclusion follows, rather than saddling the theory with thicker or more controversial premises. It is instructive to learn that the theory will work even if more demanding conditions are not satisfied. Rawls explicitly says that such is his strategy. Locke, who incorporates benevolence into the basis of his theory, thus has in one sense a weaker theory than Rawls's: it will work only in special circumstances that may or may not obtain. My theory in effect returns to Locke's richer starting point because I believe that we need it to reach a conclusion that adequately includes and supports people with disabilities. It should be granted that using thicker and more controversial premises, requiring a moderate degree of sociability and altruism, puts pressure on the theory not only to show that it can prevail in a nation of real people but also to find mechanisms to educate people who will respond well to its demands. My current focus on questions of political motivation and emotion is the natural consequence of that pressure.

The question of disability is a vast one, for the cognitive and physical impairments that "people with disabilities" have throughout their lives are similar in degree and kind to the disabilities that "normal" human beings experience as they age. As more people live longer, every country will face a burgeoning problem of disability. Sometimes the entire lifetime of a person with a disability is shorter than the period of disability in the life of a "normal" adult. So the problem of disability is vast, affecting virtually every family in every society.

One aspect of this problem is that of supporting the capabilities of people with disabilities on a basis of equal respect: What social and economic support, what forms of work adjustment, what civil and political rights, would be required to treat such people as full equals? An area of current scholarship focuses on this set of questions.

The other key aspect is thinking about care work. Disability, like childhood, requires a great human investment in care. Currently, a good deal of this work is being done by women, and much of it without pay, as if it were the natural result of love. Care labor is therefore a large source of gender-based inequality, as women are handicapped in other areas of life by the work they are doing in the home. Solving the problem has several aspects: the public sphere needs to support family and medical leave and in-home nursing care, and nations' health plans need to find some reasonable way of addressing the politically tricky issue of care at the end of life. Workplaces need to become more flexible, recognizing the demands both women and men are facing at home: flexible scheduling, tele-commuting, and other forms of adjustment need to be confronted without panic. Finally, greater reciprocity between women and men needs to develop, and society needs new conceptions of masculinity that do not deem unmanly such acts as washing the body of an aged mother or father.

Education

At the heart of the Capabilities Approach since its inception has been the importance of education. Education (in schools, in the family, in programs for both child and adult development run by nongovernmental organizations) forms people's existing capacities into developed *internal capabilities* of many kinds. This formation is valuable in itself and a source of lifelong satisfaction. It is also piv-otal to the development and exercise of many other human capabil-ities: a "fertile functioning" of the highest importance in addressing disadvantage and inequality. People who have received even a basic education have greatly enhanced employment options, chances for political participation, and abilities to interact productively with others in society, on a local, national, and even global level. For ex-ample, women who are literate are able to communicate politically with other women who face similar problems; they are no longer isolated. And these advantages lead to yet others: because education is a source of employment options and political power, it enhances a woman's bargaining position in the household, enabling her, for example, to stand up better to threats and violence, or to leave if she does not succeed in making needed changes. Because education alters the power dynamics in the household, it also opens up opportunities for a fairer distribution of household labor and thus time for leisure. Other interventions enhancing women's capabilities (credit and property rights, for example) are also fertile in similar ways, but education does seem to have special salience in the efforts nations have made to promote human equality over the past two centuries.

India has given education the status of a fundamental right of the individual. *Mohini Jain,* a key court case leading to the constitutional amendment guaranteeing that right, argues, "The dignity of Man is Inviolable . . . It is primarily education that brings forth the dignity of man." The right is held to be basic to a "dignified enjoyment of life" and (citing the Universal Declaration of Human Rights) to involve "the full development of the human personality." The other key case, *Unnikrishnan,* argues, "The right to education flows directly from the right to life and is related to the dignity of the individual."

The United States has never given education the status of a fundamental right at the national level, though some state constitutions have done so. Education does, however, enjoy a privileged position in federal constitutional law. One key case, *Plyler v. Doe*—dealing with a law that denied education to the children of illegal immigrants—asserted the importance of education in terms that refer directly to human capabilities. The discussion of education begins with a fundamental assertion of the equality of persons: "The Equal Protection Clause was intended to work nothing less than the abolition of all caste-based and invidious class-based legislation." Public education, the majority then wrote, has a "pivotal role in maintaining the fabric of our society and in sustaining our political and cultural heritage." Deprivation of education "takes an inestimable toll on the social, economic, intellectual, and psychological well-being of the individual, and poses an obstacle to individual achievement." Later these points are elaborated. Education is "necessary to prepare citizens to participate effectively and intelligently in our open political system if we are to preserve freedom and independence." It is also crucial to individual opportunity and self-development: "Illiteracy is an enduring disability. The inability to read and write will handicap the individual deprived of a basic education each and every day of his life. The inestimable toll of that deprivation on the social, economic, intellectual, and psychological well-being of the individual, and the obstacle it poses to individual achievement, make it most difficult to reconcile the cost or the principle of a status-based denial of basic education with the framework of equality embodied in the Equal Protection Clause." In effect, the opinion sees the equal right to educational benefits as inherent in the equal dignity of persons, given the pivotal role of education in securing human development and opportunity.

In both India and the United States, then, as in many other nations, education has been seen to be particularly central to human dignity, equality, and opportunity. If these connections are plausible, as they seem to be, then education deserves a key role in the Capabilities Approach.

The measures that go into the Human Development Index accordingly factor in education along with longevity, urging all nations to consider educational attainment one of the most crucial elements of their national success. Sen's profound commitment to educational advancement is shown by the fact that he devoted the entirety of his Nobel Prize money to setting up a trust (called the Pratichi Trust, named after his mother's house in Santiniketan, the town where Tagore founded his famous school) to study and advance education in West Bengal, his home state. The Pratichi Trust is a research organization, not a branch of policy-making, but its scathing reports on educational shortfalls in the state shined a national and international spotlight on the failures of local government. In particular, its emphasis on such corrupt practices as teacher absenteeism and "private tuition" (teachers tutoring affluent students for pay after school) has already generated some movement toward reform: the powerful and formerly indolent teachers' union has now taken a stand against these practices.

Understandably, and to some extent rightly, the emphasis of these interventions has been on basic literacy and numeracy; and it is surely right to think that when these skills are absent many avenues of opportunity are closed. It is important, however, not to confine the analysis of education and capabilities to those skills. A true education for human development requires much more. Currently, most modern nations, anxious about national profit and eager to seize or keep a share in the global market, have focused increasingly on a narrow set of marketable skills that are seen as having the potential to generate short-term profit. The skills associated with the humanities and the arts—critical thinking, the ability to imagine and to understand another person's situation from within, and a grasp of world history and the current global economic order—are all essential for responsible democratic citizenship, as well as for a wide range of other capabilities that people might choose to exercise in later life. Users of the Capabilities Approach need to attend carefully to issues of both pedagogy and content, asking how both the substance of studies and the nature of classroom interactions (for example, the role given to critical thinking and to imagining in daily study of material of many types) fulfill the aims inherent in the approach, particularly with regard to citizenship. (Of course education for citizenship is not simply for people who are already citizens of the nation in which they reside: the children of legal and illegal immigrants have a right to an education that prepares the same adult capabilities as those prepared for citizens.)

Education is one area in which the usual deference to choice is relaxed: governments will be well advised to require functioning of children, not simply capability. Why is this case different from most? It is different only when we are thinking about children, whose choice capabilities are immature and who may face parental pressure to work rather than to study, since they are economically dependent on their parents and have few exit options. Education is such a pivotal factor in opening up a wide range of adult capabilities that making it compulsory in childhood is justified by the dramatic expansion of capabilities in later life. Where children are concerned, then, the state's commitment to the future capabilities of its citizens, together with its strong interest in having informed and capable citizens, justifies an aggressive approach: compulsory primary and secondary education, up to at least the age of sixteen, plus ample support and encouragement for higher education. (Children are also treated asymmetrically in areas such as health and bodily integrity: we should tolerate less deference to individual—or parental—choice here than in the case of adults.) When we are dealing with the education of adults who want more education than they have had, persuasion is the correct approach.

Good education requires sensitivity to context, history, and cultural and economic circumstances. A lot of the good work in this area, like that of the Pratichi Trust, must therefore continue to be highly detailed and focused on local issues. By contrast, the goal of creating young adults who are free to engage with life in a wide range of ways has been studied all over the world for hundreds of years, and leading education theorists in many different nations have consulted with one another (Rabindranath Tagore in India with Maria Montessori in Italy and Leonard Elmhirst in Britain, for example). So it is not unreasonable to think that a cross-cultural dialogue, here as in the Capabilities Approach more generally, may yield general principles that can then be flexibly implemented in each nation and region.

Animal Entitlements

Any approach based on the idea of promoting capabilities will need to make a fundamental decision: Whose capabilities count? Virtually every proponent of the approach holds that all human beings count, and count as equals. Beyond this, there are five basic positions one may take:

1. Only human capabilities count as ends in themselves, although other capabilities may turn out to be instrumentally valuable in the promotion of human capabilities.
2. Human capabilities are the primary focus, but since human beings form relationships with nonhuman creatures, those creatures may enter into the description of the goal to be promoted, not simply as means, but as members of intrinsically valuable relationships.
3. The capabilities of all sentient creatures count as ends in them-

selves, and all should attain capabilities above some specified threshold.

4. The capabilities of all living organisms, including plants, should count, but as individual entities, not as parts of ecosystems.

5. The individualism of 1–4 is dropped: the capabilities of systems (ecosystems in particular, but also species) count as ends in themselves.

People interested in the Capabilities Approach may take any of these five positions, and time ought to produce a vigorous debate among them. Sen has taken no overall stance on these issues, although he is concerned with animal well-being and environmental quality. In *Women and Human Development*, I took position 2: relationships with other species and the world of nature are a human capability, but one in which the other entities count not merely instrumentally but also as parts of that relationship. This position was an uncomfortable half-way point between position 1 (defended by many people who have intense concern for human suffering) and a position such as 3 or 4 (defended by many others who focus, as well, on the good of other creatures).

In *Frontiers of Justice* I defend position 3, at least where social justice is concerned. I argue that the idea of social justice is inherently bound up with at least minimal sentience (the capacity to experience pain, especially) and with the accompanying capacity for striving and some type of agency. Intuitively, it seems to me that the idea of doing injustice to an animal makes sense in much the way that the idea of doing injustice to a human being makes sense: both can experience pain and harm, and both are attempting to live and act, projects that can be wrongly thwarted. The notion of justice is conceptually bound up with the idea of experienced harm and thwarting, or so I believe. Thus it seems odd, at least to me, to suggest that a tree can suffer injustice—although of course there may be other moral reasons, or reasons of a nonmoral kind, that make it wrong to damage a tree. Similarly, an ecosystem is not a center of experience and does not have a life-project or striving, so it seems odd to suggest that an ecosystem suffers *injustice*, although it may suffer many types of damage, and although there may be reasons, both moral and nonmoral (intellectual, scientific, economic) for caring about that damage. Such intuitions are difficult to articulate, and only time and future debate will more clearly map this complicated terrain. That animals can suffer not just pain but also injustice seems, however, secure.

The preceding argument suggests that, where justice is concerned, the living individual, not the species, is the locus of concern. Species may have instrumental importance to the health of individuals, and they may also have aesthetic, intellectual, and other types of ethical significance. It seems inaccurate, however, to say that the extinction of a species is an *injustice*—apart from the fact that this extinction usually proceeds by way of wrongful harms to individual species members.

The Capabilities Approach seems well suited to address the wrongs suffered by animals at the hands of humans. Utilitarians have made important contributions in this area, but the general shortcomings of their theory—its commitment to aggregation across lives and across elements of lives, its neglect of adaptive preferences—are handicaps in this area as well. Although committed utilitarians like Peter Singer usually insist that the utilitarian calculus will forbid us to inflict suffering on animals, this is an empirical matter, since humans derive a lot of pleasure (and employment) from the food business. As with slavery, the whole matter of decent treatment is made to rest on too fragile an empirical foundation. Certainly the theory would permit horrendous cruelty to a small number of animals for the sake of human well-being. As for aggregation across lives: animals pursue not simply the avoidance of pain but lives with many distinct components, including movement, friendship, and honor or dignity. It seems important to retain a sense of the separate importance of each of these elements. Finally, there is the problem of numbers. If the utilitarian considers not average but total utility, the theory can justify bringing large numbers of creatures into the world who have very miserable lives (but just above the level of not being worth living at all), since that is a way of augmenting the world's total well-being. But something like this is what the food industry does, and we object to this because we think that it is wrong to inflict a painful life on any creature, even if that life is just barely worth living.

More generally, the Capabilities Approach sees animals as agents, not as receptacles of pleasure or pain. This deep conceptual difference can help the approach develop a more pertinent sort of respect for animal striving and animal activity.

The Capabilities Approach can thus recognize the very courageous contributions of Bentham, Mill, Peter Singer, and other utilitarians to the animal-treatment debate, while insisting that a different theory does better. As for theories in the Kantian tradition: although Kant himself does not have very useful things to say about animal well-being (he thinks the only reason not to be cruel to animals is that it will encourage us not to be cruel to humans), philosopher Christine Korsgaard has recently shown that an approach rooted in the Kantian tradition can generate many of the same results as does the Capabilities Approach. The idea is that, according to Kant, we have reasons to promote not simply our own agency but also those aspects of our animality that are inherent in the ways in which we strive and act in the world: our animal nature, briefly put. But if we show respect to those (animal) aspects of ourselves, it is simply inconsistent, and a kind of vicious self-promoting of a sort to which Kantians are especially opposed, to refuse the same respect to our fellow creatures. Korsgaard's approach is still somewhat more anthropocentric than I would myself favor: according to Korsgaard, it is because of something about *us*, and animals' resemblance to *us*, that we should show them respect, not because of something about *them*. Other questions need to be raised concerning the extent to which Korsgaard's Kantian view of agency could become the source of political principles in a pluralistic society. (Korsgaard does not raise this question, since she is proposing an ethical, not a political, view.) The "bottom line" of my detailed comparison of our two positions, however, is that they are very similar and come to similar conclusions.

What are those conclusions? First, we must modify the Capabilities Approach to make it suitable for these purposes. We need an expanded notion of *dignity*, since we now need to talk not only about lives in accordance with human dignity but also about lives that are worthy of the dignity of a wide range of sentient creatures. Unlike expanded Kantian approaches, which see duties to treat animals well as derivative from duties to support our own human animality, the Capabilities Approach regards each type of animal as having a dignity all its own; the duty to respect that dignity is not derivative from duties to ourselves. Although duties, as in the human case, are first and foremost duties to individuals, the species plays a role in giving us a sense of a characteristic form of life that ought to be promoted. The capabilities list, suitably broadened, still contains the main items that we should favor, but we should be attentive to the form of life of each species, and promote, for each, the opportunity to live and act according to that species' form of life. Although choice is favored wherever the creature has a capacity for choice, a focus on functioning (a kind of sensitive paternalism) will be more appropriate in this case than in the human case.

As for the idea that we should leave animals alone when they live in "the wild," this naively romantic naturalism ought to be rejected for today's world. There is no habitat that is not pervasively affected by human action. Pretending that elephants in Africa are "in the wild" is just a way of avoiding the fact that their habitat has been encroached upon by human plans. Moreover, the only way to allow them to have a decent shot at living well is to continue intervening, but to do so wisely, not foolishly. (One form of intervention into nature that seems crucial is animal contraception. This will mean, for animals, modifying the capability list where reproductive choice is concerned. While the first priority must be the protection of habitats, even current habitats, well protected, cannot support expanding animal populations. The alternative to contraception, the introduction of predator species, seems much worse, from the point of view of animal capabilities, than enforced contraception.)

The main conclusion of my approach is that all animals are entitled to a threshold level of opportunity for a life characteristic of their kind. Whether this means a total ban on the killing of animals for food may be debated. (Both Bentham and Singer have denied this.) The painless killing of an animal of a species that does not make plans extending into the future may not be a harm: this depends on how we think about the harm of death. Therefore, some authors deeply committed to animal well-being are prepared to countenance such painless killings, if the animal has had a decent life in good conditions. At any rate, this is a point open for further debate.

What is not open for debate is the fact that the factory food industry inflicts great injustices and should be ended, as should hunting and fishing for sport, cruel practices associated with product testing, and non-necessary harm to animals in research. As for research using animal subjects that is currently necessary to improve both animal and human lives, we should say of this what we said about tragic conflict earlier: we are faced with a choice between two evils, and what we must do is to move as rapidly as possible to a state of the world in which we will not be faced with that choice. We should try to find other ways to do the research—through computer simulation, for example. Artificial meat is already being developed (not veggie-burgers, but meat synthesized from stem cells); this, too, can be a large contributor to a more just world.

Environmental Quality

No matter what position we take on the five choices outlined above, the quality of the environment clearly plays a role in the Capabilities Approach. We do not need to move beyond position 1 to argue that the quality of the natural environment and the health of ecosystems are crucial for human well-being. This is particularly true if we think of human well-being as including commitments to future generations. That vital issue has been extensively addressed in liberal political theory (for example, by Rawls), but the Capabilities Approach has not yet exhaustively pursued the topic. Getting clear about how to count the interests of subsequent generations of humans is of the highest importance for future work if the approach is to be a serious player in the environmental arena, especially since the question of counting and discounting has been so well explored in studies of risk and uncertainty, as well as related areas of environmental economics. Environmental quality would be important even if our only goal were to support the capabilities of people currently living, but the argument becomes much more powerful when future generations are taken into account in some way. So it is important to determine the right way to do this—a challenge for future workers.

Important recent work by Breena Holland has shown that in confronting the questions of environmental quality and sustainability, the Capabilities Approach offers distinct advantages over other approaches currently favored in environmental economics—in large part because it encourages the disaggregated consideration of a wide range of effects on different parts of human lives. For example, considering impacts on health separately from impacts on the economy is important, since a single-minded focus on economic growth might lead to the choice of policies that somewhat reduce average health status.

Holland's is a purely anthropocentric approach, treating environmental quality as instrumental to human life quality—not because she necessarily believes that this approach is a fully correct one, but because, in the context of public debate, it is useful to show that very strong conclusions can be generated from premises that are weak and uncontroversial, premises that most of the public can be presumed to accept. At the other end of the spectrum of possible approaches, it is easy enough to see that a position that treats ecosystems as ends in themselves, apart from the individuals in them, could generate strong conclusions with respect to environmental protection. Few people hold those positions, however, so arguments of this sort are not likely to have an impact on policy choice. (I myself reject those positions because I believe that sentient individuals, animals and humans, have value for their own sake, not as a part of some larger system, and that larger systems are valuable as supports for individual lives.) I believe that over time it will be possible, through arguments emphasizing the suffering of animals and the value of their lives, to move many people to the middle of the spectrum, developing an "overlapping consensus" concerning the view that animal capabilities matter for their own sake. Such a consensus, however, does not currently exist. Therefore, since action protecting the environment is not a matter on which we can afford to wait, it is important to develop anthropocentric positions like Holland's as effectively as possible. Other capability theorists, however, are doing good work exploring a range of different positions.

The question of environmental quality is closely linked to the question of population control. That issue has been at the forefront of Sen's work for some time. Sen rejects the dire predictions of Malthusians that we are facing an imminently impending food catastrophe. He does, however, favor major efforts to curb population growth. This policy issue intersects with the theoretical core of the Capabilities Approach, because many proponents of population control have favored coercive strategies that greatly reduce human freedom of choice. China, and India under Indira Gandhi, moved aggressively in this direction. Is this a tragic dilemma, in which life and health are pitted against areas of freedom to choose? Sen doubts that this is so, because he is (tentatively) convinced by the evidence that empowering women (through education, employment options, credit, and so on) is more effective in reducing population than are coercive strategies. At any rate, even if coercive strategies were similar in effect, the intrinsic worth of freedom should tilt our choice in the direction of the empowerment model. Sen observes that the Indian state of Kerala has managed population control very effectively by relying on education and empowerment, and that this model is both more efficient (probably) than the Chinese model and ethically superior.

Constitutional Law and Political Structure

Once we argue that certain capabilities are central to the idea of a life worthy of human dignity, and once we accept a conception of the task of society's "basic structure" (its basic political principles together with the institutional structure that embodies them) as involving at least the securing of a minimum level of the Central Capabilities, it is natural to ask how a political structure can indeed secure them. Sen's work on the Capabilities Approach makes little reference to law and to institutional structures within democracy, although it suggests some obvious directions for public policy. For my work, focused as it has been on the question of minimal social justice, law and political structure have been central from the beginning. I envisage the account of Central Capabilities and of the threshold as a source of political principles that can be translated into a set of (minimally) just political institutions. I have particularly connected the capabilities list to the part of a nation's written constitution (or of its unwritten constitutional principles, if it has no written constitution) that elaborates citizens' fundamental entitlements. Many nations by now enumerate entitlements in a way that connects them to the idea of a life worthy of human dignity: the constitutional traditions of India and South Africa are particularly interesting to study in this respect.

Recently, I have been engaged in work that makes the connection of the Capabilities Approach to constitutional law even clearer, and I have offered a set of capability-based templates for the work of the U.S. Supreme Court. Several decades of admirable progress in protecting human capabilities have recently been followed by a sharp turn of the Supreme Court toward what I call "obtuse formalism," an approach that focuses on technical legal argument without serious engagement with capabilities, even those securely grounded in the constitutional text, hence with disadvantage. A full-scale investigation of the relationship of the Capabilities Approach to constitutional law would require detailed investigation of each concrete area of human capability, as law has specified it through both constitutional text and an ongoing history of judicial interpretation.

Is there a conceptual link between the idea of Central Capabilities and the task of government? Entitlements, in my view, are correlative with duties: if people have entitlements, then there is a duty to secure them, even if it is difficult to say to whom the duty belongs. I argue that the whole world is under a collective obligation to secure the capabilities to all world citizens, even if there is no worldwide political organization. How to assign the duties to specific groups and individuals is a difficult matter, and one requiring interdisciplinary theoretical cooperation, since history and political science offer important insights about changing global structures. The difficulty is greatest in the global context, where there is no state and no good reasons to think that we ought to have a single overarching state. Even here, many of the duties to secure human capabilities are assigned to nations; but some belong, as well, to NGOs, to corporations, to international organizations, and to individuals. In that sense the duties are ethical rather than political: they do not require a state enforcement mechanism to be morally binding.

Nonetheless, rights (or the Central Capabilities) have no conceptual connection to government action. A long tradition, beginning in the West at least with Aristotle, has argued that a key task of government, and a reason for the existence of government, is to secure to people their most central entitlements. As the U.S. Declaration of Independence puts it, recapitulating a long tradition of argument, "to secure these rights, Governments are instituted among Men, deriving their just powers from the consent of the governed"—and any government that fails to secure basic entitlements has failed in its most essential task. If a capability really belongs on the list, then governments have the obligation to protect and secure it, using law and public policy to achieve this end. The world context is unique, because there is no overarching state, and thus none that can be shown unjust because it fails to perform this task, although it would be right to say that the collective structure of world institutions has produced injustice and should be changed. When we are thinking of a specific nation-state, however, we are entitled to ask whether it has secured the Central Capabilities to its people. If it has not, it is not even minimally just.

Sen attempts to avoid granting a conceptual connection between capabilities and government by citing examples of capabilities (rights) that should not be legally enforced, such as the right of a family member to be consulted in all family decisions. Of this example I would say: either such conduct is required by a notion of a life worthy of human dignity or it is not. If it is, then it ought to be legally enforced (just as we legally enforce prohibitions on child abuse and domestic violence). If it is not, then it does not belong on a list of Central Capabilities or human rights. If we do put something on that list we connect it, both practically and conceptually, to the idea of the purposes for which "governments were instituted among men." My own view is that the right he mentions—that of family members to be consulted in decision-making—is a matter concerning which citizens may reasonably disagree, given differences in their comprehensive doctrines, religious and ethical. Some religious and ethical views emphasize family solidarity and transparency; others insist on a higher degree of autonomy for the individual. Where these deep differences exist, consultation (the policy of just one group of religious and ethical views) should not be coercively enforced; so I agree with Sen about the example. But by the same token the right of a family member to be consulted would not belong on my list of Central Capabilities, which is defined as a political conception of human capability that is the potential object of an overlapping consensus among all the reasonable comprehensive doctrines.

The ten capabilities, then, are *goals* that fulfill or correspond to people's prepolitical entitlements: thus we say of people that they are entitled to the ten capabilities on the list. In the context of a nation, it then becomes the job of government to secure them, if that government is to be even minimally just. In effect, then, the presence of entitlements gives governments a job to do, and a central job of government will be to secure the capabilities to people. The existence of human and animal lives gives a reason for governments to exist and generates obligations of a distinctly political kind. When, in the case of the whole world, we decide that an overarching single government might not be the best way of solving problems of capability-failure in poorer nations, government still plays a major role in securing them: the government of the poorer nations, in the first place, and, in the second place, the governments of richer nations, which have obligations to assist the poorer. Giving people what they are entitled to have, by virtue of their humanity, is a major reason for governments to exist, and a major job they have once they do.

When a given capability has been recognized as a fundamental entitlement in a nation's constitution (usually at a somewhat abstract level), much more work needs to be done. The capability will need further elaboration or specification, and the threshold will have to be correctly set. Let us briefly consider just one major capability, in order to see how a constitutional tradition performs such a task.

The history of the U.S. constitutional tradition regarding the "free exercise of religion" provides a nice example of how a Central Human Capability, abstractly specified at the outset, can be implemented through constitutional law over time, with a deepening and incrementally specific understanding of its requirements. At the time of the constitutional framing, the Framers considered several different sorts of language for what they wanted to protect under this heading, but they settled on the following wording: "Congress shall make no law respecting an establishment of religion, or prohibiting the free exercise thereof." For the present I shall leave our "Establishment Clause" to one side in order to focus on the "Free Exercise Clause."

The problem the Framers knew well, by that time, was that religious liberty is always at risk when a majority of citizens belong to a particular religion. Both belief and conduct, on the part of minorities, is likely to be infringed—sometimes maliciously, but sometimes also heedlessly, as when a majority selects Sunday as the day off from work, ignoring the predicament of those whose holy day is Saturday; or when a majority passes laws for compulsory military service, ignoring the fact that some religions enjoin pacifism; or when a majority allows alcohol (associated with Christian ritual) to remain legal but restricts hallucinogenic drugs, ignoring the fact that hallucinogens are an important part of religious ritual in some minority religions.

In such cases, the idea of "free exercise" needs to be interpreted capaciously—this means not just striking down laws that penalize people for religious belief and practice but also looking at the problem of unequal liberty, special burdens that minorities face because of their minority choices. Because the Free Exercise Clause was not held to apply to the actions of local and state governments—where most of the action is—until the twentieth century, we have relatively few cases interpreting the clause from the early period, but we do have plenty of evidence, from state constitutions and their histories of interpretation, that the idea of religiously based "accommodation" was a widely accepted norm. That is to say, when a law generally applicable to all imposes a special burden on minority religious belief or practice, the minority in question may have a dispensation from that law unless some "compelling state interest" exists on the other side. For example, when policies involving work days burden people whose holy day is not that of the majority, the state is required to make adjustments. Policies involving drug use—for example, the use of hallucinogens in Native American and other religions—also appear to give grounds for a dispensation from general laws, although there continues to be dispute about that question. The classic compelling governmental interest that may be invoked to justify a "substantial burden" is an interest in peace and safety, though other state interests, such as education, have at times been recognized as justifying a burden on religious practice. Administrative burdens must be extreme to constitute a compelling state interest, but the refusal of a Native American family to allow their child to have a Social Security number was found to involve such a weighty state interest. Ending racial discrimination was also held to be a compelling interest in the case in which Bob Jones University lost its tax-exempt status for its ban on interracial dating.

One canonical statement of the accommodation principle can be found in a letter from George Washington, our first president, to the Quakers about their refusal to perform military service: "I assure you very explicitly, that in my opinion the conscientious scruples of all men should be treated with great delicacy and tenderness: and it is my wish and desire, that the laws may always be as extensively accommodated to them, as a due regard for the protection and essential interests of the nation may justify and permit." Washington did not ask the Quakers to perform military service; nor did he expect them, as John Locke would have, to pay a legal penalty for their disobedience. (See *Liberty of Conscience,* chapter 2, for a contrast between Locke's view and that of Roger Williams, who favored ample accommodations for the sake of conscience.)

In the mid-twentieth century, this general idea began to be turned into the legal framework we now use to understand what it is to implement this all-important capability in a way that respects the equal worth of all citizens. Adell Sherbert was a good worker in a textile factory in South Carolina. In the 1950s, her employer added a sixth work day, and Saturday was the chosen day, since almost all workers were Christians. Mrs. Sherbert, however, was a Seventh-Day Adventist, for whom Saturday is the holy day. She was fired because she refused to come to work on Saturday, and she could not find another job, because all employers in the area had similar work days. Not surprisingly, none chose to close on Saturday and remain open on Sunday. She applied to the state for unemployment compensation but was turned down because she had refused "suitable work."

She went to court, claiming that the unemployment policy violated her religious free exercise. In 1963 the U.S. Supreme Court found, in *Sherbert v. Verner*, that the denial of benefits by the state was a violation of her constitutional right to the free exercise of her religion: they said that it was like fining someone for Saturday worship. The state, they said, is not constitutionally required to give unemployment benefits at all; once it does so, however, it may not make those benefits conditional on a person's violation of religious scruple. They then articulated a general theoretical framework for the implementation of "free exercise": no law or policy may impose a "substantial burden" on a person's religious exercise without a "compelling state interest."

Those notions are still highly abstract. The case made it clear that denying benefits to someone in a case like this was a "substantial burden," but it offered no definition of "substantial burden." The Court also rejected South Carolina's contention that the administrative difficulty of dealing with the claims of religious minorities constituted a "compelling state interest," but it offered no general account of that notion. That is the way our constitutional system works: incrementally, as the Court gradually builds a set of railroad tracks, progressively elaborating the conditions for implementing the capability in question, and gradually articulating the contours of a right. Following the full history of such cases would show us how each of those notions has been successively, and more specifically, interpreted as new cases come along. It would also show how new questions about the boundaries of this capability come forward with new cases. For example, does the free-exercise principle give parents the right to risk the health or life of their children? (Think about Jehovah's Witnesses and blood transfusions.) Can it be a "substantial burden" when the government is simply doing something with its own land, such as building a road (thus preventing Native American tribes from making certain sorts of ritual use of the land)? (In *Lyng v. Northwest Indian Cemetery*, the Court found that there was no substantial burden, even though the road disrupted the use of the land for ritual purposes—because the government owned the land, and was just using what it owned.) And, on the compelling state interest side: Is administrative burdensomeness ever a compelling state interest, if the burden is very great? Is education a compelling state interest, and, if so, what sort and amount of education? As such questions are answered, one case at a time, the contours of the capability become clearer, the railroad tracks more extensive. This image should not suggest that there is always progress: a good tradition may be rejected. It is relatively difficult to do so, however, in a system that respects precedent.

As this example makes clear, judicial implementation of a central, constitutionally recognized capability has several characteristics that we should notice in developing the approach further, since they appear to be valuable in delivering an adequate specification of a capability to people. In this sense it has a particular affinity with the Capabilities Approach. First, the capability in question is treated *separately, as something of importance in its own right*. Although at times the Court will look across to other rights, expressing a view that protection in one area is necessary for protection in another, this is a relatively rare occurrence. The Free Exercise and Establishment Clauses do have an interlocking history of implementation, but that is because these are understood to form part of a single set of guarantees in the area of religion. Even the Free Speech Clause of the same amendment has a more or less completely separate interpretive history.

It is certainly true that capabilities form an interlocking set of entitlements, and that some capabilities may be pivotal in promoting others. The constitutional tradition is able to recognize this, while implicitly rejecting any sort of commensuration among the fundamental entitlements, as well as any type of compensation that would buy off one entitlement with quantities of another. A deficit in religious liberty and equality cannot be atoned for in any other coin. George Washington did not say to the Quakers, "We'll make you serve in the army, but we'll give you a handsome cash payment for so doing." In *People v. Philips*, a Catholic priest who refused to answer, under oath, information that came to him in the confessional was not told, "Answer, and we'll make it up to you by giving a nice donation to your church." Instead he was told that "the mild and just principles" of the law would never put someone in "such a horrible dilemma" by forcing him to choose between violating his religious scruples and going to prison: "The only course is, for the court to declare that he shall not testify . . . at all." We can see why: the priest was being asked to violate his conscience, and it was held that this violation was tantamount to abolishing the sacrament of the confessional. This problem would not have gone away had the priest, or his church, received a handsome cash donation. It just doesn't work to say, "Confess your secrets to your priest, secure in the knowledge that, should he have to divulge them in court, your church will get a handsome cash donation."

The second feature of judicial implementation that these examples illustrate is its cautious *incrementalism,* building up a structure through the years, as one case advances upon, or confirms and deepens the insights of, another case. Often the contours of an abstractly specified right are exceedingly unclear at the outset. (The U.S. Free Speech principle, for example, was long understood in such a way as not to protect the speech of dissidents during wartime.) As time goes on and new cases come forward, we understand more clearly what we are protecting, and the protection is nailed down more firmly. Thus the abstract idea of a "threshold" becomes the idea of increasingly specific definitions of constitutional language and of the interpretive language ("substantial burden," "compelling state interest") that has been used to articulate it.

A third related feature is the *contextualism* of good interpretation. Abstract principles are always realized in a concrete context. A realistic sense of that context and the opportunities it affords is absolutely crucial to the correct adjudication of cases involving Central Capabilities. Judges cannot afford to remain at the level of generality or to take refuge in an approach that is merely formalistic, refusing to consider the content of each case: they need to dig into history and social reality in order to face the hard question of whether a given capability has really been secured to people. Contextualism here does not mean an ad hoc "situation ethics" that offers no guidance for the future, or a rootless pragmatism: demanding general principles are being implemented. In order to implement them well, however, we must understand how people really operate in the specific areas of life in which opportunity is either open or closed to them. Contextualism is a desideratum for all approaches, but it has a particular affinity with the Capabilities Approach, which has always emphasized the importance of examining each person's story in its social and historical context, in order to discern hidden obstacles to full capability.

A fourth feature of good judicial interpretation of a constitutional right is its constant *focus on the rights of minorities to equal treatment*. Indeed the judicial role is rightly focused on such cases, because minorities are at a disadvantage in the majoritarian political process, and thus their entitlements especially need judicial protec-

tion. We can barely imagine a First Amendment Free Exercise liti-
gant from the Presbyterian or Episcopal Church—what problems
would they be likely to have? The majority makes the rules, and so it
is minorities who are unequally at risk of suffering a "substantial
burden." In fact, one fine thing about the tradition is that it reads,
at times, like a seminar in minority understanding. At first, the U.S.
Supreme Court had difficulty understanding any religion that is
not like Protestantism; thus Catholics and Jews did relatively well,
but Native Americans, and most certainly Mormons, did relatively
badly.

As time goes on, however, the very shape of the tradition dictates
that the Court will repeatedly consider the tenets and claims of un-
familiar traditions and will learn more and more about what consti-
tutes a burden in these cases. Native American religion is now much
better understood than it was in the early days; a community-based
religion such as the Old Order Amish is treated quite fairly. My own
personal favorite is *Swann v. Pack,* a case from Tennessee involving
a sect that handled poisonous snakes. The question was whether
there was a compelling state interest in avoiding the danger posed
by these snakes. In the process of answering this question, the Court
went into a most humble and interesting disquisition on the sect,
its views about snakes, the centrality of snakes to the sect's worship,
and so on—concluding that there was a substantial burden if the
most dangerous snakes were disallowed. At one point, a lower court
found that if children were excluded there was no compelling state
interest in restricting the practice in question. A higher court (in
this case the Supreme Court of the state of Tennessee) ruled the
other way, citing risks to adults who had not been fully informed of
the danger. But still, the sense of deference and sensitivity to a very
small and atypical minority is extremely striking.

So far, then, my work on capabilities and law has focused some-what narrowly on the protection of fundamental rights in a written constitution and its implementation through judicial interpreta-tion. This focus is not adequate, since it presupposes, first, a politi-cal structure in which the task of interpreting fundamental entitle-ments has already been assigned to the judiciary, and second, a confidence that they do this job well. But fundamental capabilities are implemented in other ways: through legislation and through administrative agencies. The voluminous literature on public choice has yielded significant results about such questions as the role of interest groups in promoting or opposing programs of change and the role of certain key elements of political structure—voting proce-dures, bicameralism, federalism, judicial review itself—in avoiding some of the difficulties endemic to public choice and creating a de-liberative process that is informed by normative commitments such as equal agency and reciprocity.

Sen's work within the Capabilities Approach, meanwhile, has ad-dressed this issue to some extent, by focusing on the intrinsic and instrumental value of democracy and public debate. By contrast to opponents who characterize a commitment to public rationality as "Western," Sen, in his book *The Argumentative Indian,* as well as in *India: Democracy and Participation,* shows how deeply this commit-ment is rooted in Indian traditions. His discussion of religious ex-tremism, in *Identity and Violence,* also focuses on a failure of public discussion as one of the primary sources of group polarization and conflict, although I believe he is wrong to suggest that religious vio-lence will diminish if there is simply more public discussion (unless we carefully stipulate the structure and nature of that discussion). Sen, however, has not yet offered any detailed account of democratic procedure that would address the structural issues just mentioned.

It is not even clear whether he favors the entrenchment of fundamental rights beyond the reach of majority vote.

The empowerment of citizens through democratic procedures is a shared aim of most people working on the Capabilities Approach, and a very important feature of it, as can be seen in both Sen's and my emphasis on agency and respect for people's choices. Too frequently, however, the word "democracy" is insufficiently defined. Most modern democracies have a place for rights entrenched beyond the reach of majority vote, and I would argue that if democracy means that "the people rule," such entrenchment is a necessary feature of democracy, since it protects fundamental aspects of self-rule (such as one person, one vote; the equal protection of the laws; due process; and freedom of association). In other words, democracy should not be understood as mere majoritarianism. We can also mention that one of the most empowering measures any recent democracy has thought up has been the one-third quota for women in India's rural *panchayats,* or village councils. That measure could be said to be undemocratic if what one means is that it is favored by local majorities; often it is not. It was implemented through a constitutional amendment that is binding on all. And yet women have been empowered by it in a remarkable way.

So the word "democracy" tells us very little, and one can be all for empowerment and respect while still thinking that it's an open question how political structure ought to address these matters. We badly need to raise the whole issue of political structure and think through the problems that have been thoroughly discussed by political scientists and public choice theorists: issues such as separation of powers, voting procedure, the role of interest groups, procedures for constraining that role, and many other important topics. Reference to "democratic discussion" in the absence of a refined structural analysis—particularly when a large specialized literature on such issues exists—seems like mere hand-waving. Similarly problematic is the frequent reference to "civil society," before we examine the relationship of civil society organizations to the equality of all citizens and to fundamental constitutional norms. One of the most powerful civil society organizations in history has been the Hindu Right, which uses its immense power of mobilization to denigrate Muslims—through public discussion! Lobbying groups, similarly, are powerful civil society organizations that often work against the equal empowerment of all citizens. So much more needs to be said: none of these loci of discussion is good in itself.

A major challenge for the Capabilities Approach in the future, then, is to think more systematically about political structure. To some extent this cannot be done in abstraction from each nation's history and circumstances (the educational level of voters, the likelihood that judges are in touch with the lives and opinions of voters, and so on). Nonetheless, the public choice literature, and the literature on deliberative and participatory democracy, show us progress on specific questions, and it seems important to connect the Capabilities Approach to that sophisticated body of work.

Capabilities and Human Psychology

An equally significant challenge for the future is to work out a political psychology—an account of the emotions and other psychological dispositions that support and impede a program of realizing human capabilities. It is obvious that people will not create a program as demanding as this one, requiring a lot of sacrifice of personal self-interest, without emotions of compassion and solidarity. Daniel Batson's important research has shown us that compassion (which he calls "empathetic concern") is not reliable on its own, because it can easily give priority to people close to the self; at the same time, it shows that emotion has a singular motivational power that we would be foolish to neglect. Institutions have a solidity and impartiality that people often don't have, and they will outlast momentary swings of sentiment. Nonetheless, if sentiments wane, the good institutions will eventually undergo a change. If justifying a set of political institutions requires showing that they can be realized by real people and be stable over time, this task cannot be completed without an inquiry into the emotional dimensions of the political sphere. It is not surprising that the topic of emotion has been central for many of the great political theorists, including Aristotle, Hobbes, Rousseau, Mill, and Rawls.

Such an inquiry needs to have two parts. First, it needs to ask what we know about human psychology "in itself," that is, whatever there is of human psychology that is not the creation of a particular culture. Human beings are not limitlessly malleable, and there are psychological studies of general human tendencies (to peer pressure, deference to authority, fear, and disgust, for example) that have robust cross-cultural credentials.

Then, second, we need to understand as well as we can how malleable these emotional tendencies are and what interventions (in the family, in schools, in other social settings) may channel them in a direction that supports the goal of realizing the Central Capabilities for all world citizens. Mill believed that people were extremely malleable, and he proposed a program of public education that was to make people identify their own success in life with the success of others, including others in the future. Mill certainly exaggerated the extent of human malleability, but we should not underrate the role of social norms in shaping emotions at all ages. A fuller understanding of the developmental process and of the ways in which a variety of social influences shapes the emotions that are relevant to politics is crucial if we want to realize the approach, or even to justify it.

Part of this task will be to understand the emotions that support the Capabilities Approach, such as compassion and respect. These are not intrinsically reliable, because they are often narrowly and unevenly felt. Thus one question before us is how we can make them support policies based on the idea of human equality without robbing them of their motivating force, and how we may educate these emotions without undermining cherished values of free speech and debate. Another large job will be to investigate emotions that subvert the Capabilities Approach, including various forms of hatred and disgust, but also including a type of primitive shame about one's own helplessness that often leads to the shaming and stigmatization of others.

When we begin to work along these lines, we need to take very seriously the limitations imposed by a commitment to political liberalism. Political liberalism asks us to show respect for the diverse views of human life that are present in a pluralistic society, by not building our political principles on any metaphysical, epistemological, or psychological doctrine that is controversial between such groups. This is difficult to do, but John Rawls has given us reason to think that it can be done, by producing politically workable versions of ideas (the person, agency, autonomy, objectivity) that are developed in divisive ways in the different religious and secular views of life. Rawls believed that something similar could be done with psychology, and he thought that it would have to be done if a reasonable account of political stability were to be given, but he did not do it. He suspended the account of child development and emotion that he had advanced in *A Theory of Justice,* suggesting that it was perhaps too controversial, and he insisted that a "reasonable political psychology" would need to be developed, but he did not do so himself.

With Rawls, I believe that the task is both important and doable, within the confines of political liberalism. In order to do it well, we must learn as much as possible about scientific and experimental studies of emotion, since those provide data-points that can presumably be accepted by all the reasonable views. The normative side (which emotions we ought to foster) will come from the political principles themselves, which presumably have already become the object of an overlapping consensus. We cannot learn all we need to learn about children, particularly very young children, from experimental data alone, however. Humanistic disciplines such as clinical psychology, psychoanalysis, history, and literature also give us insight into the dynamics of a child's inner life. It is always good when such insights are backed up by experiments, as is often the case, but experiments simply cannot tell us everything we need to know about early fear, or narcissism, or shame. So we should use insights from the humanistic and interpretive disciplines in a flexible and nondogmatic way, trying to offer our fellow citizens multiple avenues into the account: for example, someone whose world view rejects psychoanalysis may be receptive to similar insights offered by Proust.

Talking well about human emotions requires experience of human life, wide reading about a range of human predicaments, and an unusual degree of insight into both suffering and joy. Few economists have had such insight, or at least they have not demonstrated it in their work. Sometimes they have dismissed the whole topic of emotion as insignificant. Among the great philosophers, some (Plato, Aristotle, Seneca, Rousseau, Mill, and Tagore, for example) have had the sort of human insight I have in mind. Others seem to lack it—or at least they avoid writing about such matters in their work. Capability theorists need to learn all they can from experimental work in psychology, but they also need to become readers of novels, biographies, autobiographies, and psychological case histories—anything that can enhance their grasp of those complicated elements of human experience on which our hope of political achievement and stability depends.

Conclusion

We are living in an era dominated by the profit motive and by anxiety over national economic achievements. Economic growth, however, while a part of wise public policy, is just a part, and a mere instrument at that. It is people who matter ultimately; profits are only instrumental means to human lives. The purpose of global development, like the purpose of a good domestic national policy, is to enable people to live full and creative lives, developing their potential and fashioning a meaningful existence commensurate with their equal human dignity. In other words, the real purpose of development is *human development;* other approaches and measures are at best a proxy for the development of human lives, and most don't reflect human priorities in a rich, accurate, or nuanced way. The widespread use of average GDP as a measure of quality of life persists despite a growing consensus that it is not even a good proxy for human life quality.

Most nations, operating domestically, have understood that respect for people requires a richer and more complicated account of national priorities than that provided by GDP alone. On the whole, they have offered a more adequate account in their constitutions and other founding documents. But the theories that dominate

policy-making in the new global order have yet to attain the respectful complexity embodied in good national constitutions, and these
theories, defective as they are, have enormous power. Unfortunately,
they greatly influence not just international bodies but also the
domestic priorities of nations—and many nations today are pursuing economic growth in ways that shortchange other commitments
they have made to their people. The use of incomplete theories is
only one part of the story behind this narrowness of focus, but it is
a part that can be and is being resourcefully addressed.

A new theoretical paradigm is evolving, one that is the ally of people's demands for a quality of life that their equal human dignity
requires. Unlike the dominant approaches, it begins from a commitment to the equal dignity of all human beings, whatever their
class, religion, caste, race, or gender, and it is committed to the attainment, for all, of lives that are worthy of that equal dignity. Both
a comparative account of the quality of life and a theory of basic
social justice, it remedies the major deficiencies of the dominant approaches. It is sensitive to distribution, focusing particularly on the
struggles of traditionally excluded or marginalized groups. It is sensitive to the complexity and the qualitative diversity of the goals
that people pursue. Rather than trying to squeeze all these diverse
goals into a single box, it carefully examines the relationships
among them, thinking about how they support and complement
one another. It also takes account of the fact that people may need
different quantities of resources if they are to come up to the same
level of ability to choose and act, particularly if they begin from different social positions.

For all these reasons, the Capabilities Approach is attracting attention all over the world, as an alternative to dominant approaches
to development in development economics and public policy. It is

also attracting attention as an approach to basic social justice, within nations and between nations—in some ways agreeing with other philosophical theories of social justice, in some ways departing from them—for example, by giving greater support to the struggles of people with disabilities than a social contract model seems to permit.

Our world needs more critical thinking and more respectful argument. The distressingly common practice of arguing by sound bite urgently needs to be replaced by a mode of public discourse that is itself more respectful of our equal human dignity. The Capabilities Approach is offered as a contribution to national and international debate, not as a dogma that must be swallowed whole. It is laid out to be pondered, digested, compared with other approaches —and then, if it stands the test of argument, to be adopted and put into practice. What this means is that you, the readers of this book, are the authors of the next chapter in this story of human development.

POSTSCRIPT

This book tells the story of an evolving intellectual and practical movement whose professional association can be joined by anyone who cares about these ideas: the Human Development and Capability Association (HDCA). Launched in 2004 (after three years of preparatory conferences), the association holds an annual meeting, publishes a journal (the *Journal of Human Development and Capabilities*, affiliated with the UNDP but now editorially controlled by the association), and sponsors a wide range of seminars and activities all over the world. Although Amartya Sen and I are its two "founding presidents," the daily work of the association is largely sustained by its rotating executive committee, by a group of intensely dedicated younger scholars who are known as the "worker bees," and by its current president, who serves for a two-year term. (After Sen and Nussbaum, presidents have included Frances Stewart of Oxford University and Kaushik Basu of Cornell University, now Chief Economic Advisor to the Government of India.)

The goal of the association is to enable people interested in the approach to transcend some significant separations that exist in the academic world as it is currently configured:

(a) Separations between the disciplines. Economists need to talk more with political scientists, philosophers, sociologists, psychologists, environmental scientists, and others, if the promise inherent in the approach is to be realized.

(b) The separation between theory and practice. Development practitioners and politicians have a lot to offer to those doing intellectual work, and vice versa. Theoretical work should respond to the real world, and the world of public policy and development practice can be illuminated by theoretical approaches.

(c) The separation between older and younger. The academic world badly needs occasions that provide younger workers whose careers are just beginning with access to senior theorists.

(d) Separations among regions and nations. Both senior scholars and especially their younger colleagues need opportunities to meet one another across national and regional lines.

Any reader of this book, whether currently connected to an academic institution or not, can join the association, submit a paper to its annual meeting, and use its website as a way of networking with other people interested in the same issues.

APPENDIX A

APPENDIX B

CHAPTER NOTES

BIBLIOGRAPHY

ACKNOWLEDGMENTS

INDEX

Appendix A
Heckman on Capabilities

Throughout his distinguished career, the economist James J. Heckman of the University of Chicago, winner of the Nobel Prize in Economics in 2000, has focused on an idea of human capability in connection with his interest in early childhood. Heckman's important empirical and formal work has until now been insufficiently cited in work on the Human Development Approach, and the ideas embodied in his parallel research project should become central to this work in the future, since they provide clear directions for public policy in the development of human capabilities, as well as elegant formal models that illuminate the issues in question. A conference at the University of Chicago in spring 2010, organized by Heckman and Nussbaum, with Sen as the keynote speaker, began to bridge this gap, and we hope that mutual illumination will continue.

Heckman understands "capabilities" as skills or potentials for achievement. His approach is rooted in the "human capital" approach within economics, and, definitionally, his notion of capability is closer to Nussbaum's notion of "internal capability" than to her notion of "combined capability." In other words, the external social circumstances that either permit the choice of functioning or inhibit it are not, as such, elements of a given capability, as Heckman uses the term. Thus good communication between the two approaches requires attention to issues of translation.

Heckman's central contention (drawing on a wide range of psychological research and other empirical studies) is that human capabilities are shaped decisively at a very early age by environmental influences of a wide variety, beginning with prenatal influences on later development, and continuing through early life in the family and early schooling. Heckman is interested in both cognitive skills and what he calls "noncognitive" skills, by which he means emotional and characterological abilities (attentiveness, self-control, and so on) that strongly influence adult success. (I have placed the word "noncognitive" in quotes because it is no part of Heckman's program to defend a noncognitive conception of emotions as against a cognitive conception; he uses the term only to distinguish the emotional realm from the realm of calculative and other intellectual skills.) Empirical studies show that early intervention is crucial, building the case for preschool interventions and programs that partner with families in seeking to develop potential in a society riven by inequality. Indeed, Heckman contends that a great deal of human potential is being wasted by the failure to intervene early, both through programs designed to enhance the future human being's health *in utero* and through programs after birth. Although research shows that most central human abilities are decisively affected by what happens at a very young age, Heckman also argues that some key emotional abilities, such as self-control, develop later, up through adolescence, thus giving reasons to devise supportive programs for those ages as well.

Heckman continues a broad-based research program in collaboration with psychologists, health experts, and family specialists.

This work needs to be fully integrated into the work of philosophers and economists pursuing the Human Development paradigm. The following key publications of Heckman and his co-authors are a small sample of their work on human capabilities, but they contain references to related studies by Heckman and others:

Borghans, Lex, Angela Lee Duckworth, James J. Heckman, and Bas ter Weel. "The Economics and Psychology of Personality Traits." *Journal of Human Resources* 43 (2006): 972–1058.

Borghans, Lex, Bart H. H. Golsteyn, James J. Heckman, and Huub Meijers. "Gender Differences in Risk Aversion and Ambiguity Aversion." *Journal of the European Economic Association* 7 (2009): 649–658.

Carneiro, Pedro, and James J. Heckman. "Human Capital Policy." IZA Discussion Paper no. 821, SSRN http://ssrn.com/abstract = 434544.

Cunha, Flavio, and James J. Heckman. "Formulating, Identifying and Estimating the Technology of Cognitive and Noncognitive Skill Formation." *Journal of Human Resources* 43 (2006): 738–782.

———. "The Technology of Skill Formation." *AEA Papers and Proceedings* 97 (May 2007): 31–47.

———. "The Economics and Psychology of Inequality and Human Development." *Journal of the European Economics Association* 7 (2009): 320–364.

Cunha, Flavio, James J. Heckman, Lance Lochner, and Dimitriy V. Masterov. "Interpreting the Evidence on Life Cycle Skill Formation." *Handbook of the Economics of Education*, vol. 1, ed. Eric A. Hanushek and Finis Welch. Amsterdam: Elsevier, 2006, 697–812.

Heckman, James J. "Catch 'em Young." *Wall Street Journal*, January 10, 2006, p. A14.

———. "Skill Formation and the Economics of Investing in Disadvantaged Children." *Science* 312, June 30, 2006, 1900–1902.

———. "The Economics, Technology, and Neuroscience of Human Capability Formation." *PNAS* 104, August 14, 2007, 13250–13255.

———. "Schools, Skills, and Synapses." *Economic Inquiry* 46 (2008): 289–324.

——. "Schools, Skills, and Synapses." VOX, http://www.voxeu.org/index/php?q=node/1564.

Heckman, James J., and Dimitriy V. Masterov. "The Productivity Argument for Investing in Young Children." *Review of Agricultural Economics* 29 (2007): 446–493.

Heckman, James J., and Yona Rubinstein. "The Importance of Noncognitive Skills: Lessons from the GED Testing Program." *American Economic Review* 91 (2001): 145–149.

Heckman, James J., Jora Stixrud, and Sergio Urzua. "The Effects of Cognitive and Noncognitive Abilities on Labor Market Outcomes and Social Behavior." *Journal of Labor Economics* 24 (2006): 411–482.

Knudsen, Eric I., James J. Heckman, Judy L. Cameron, and Jack P. Shonkoff. "Economic, Neurobiological, and Behavioral Perspectives on Building America's Future Workforce." *PNAS* 103 (2006): 10155–10162.

APPENDIX B
SEN ON WELL-BEING AND AGENCY

In Sen's Dewey Lectures, "Well-Being, Agency, and Freedom," *Journal of Philosophy* 82 (1985), 169–221, he employs a distinction between *well-being freedom* and *agency freedom* that has had considerable influence. Since I do not use this distinction (nor does Sen in his most recent work), it is important to say why not, and to work out the relationship between Sen's categories and my own.

Sen distinguishes between the "well-being aspect" of a person—by which he apparently means that person's flourishing, or life going well—from the "agency aspect," the power of choice that he associates with Kantian moral philosophy. He then, however, surveys a variety of conceptions of well-being, rejecting both mental-state conceptions and desire-satisfaction conceptions, arguing that they are too narrow: they do not include other important aspects of a person's well-being, prominently including various forms of activity. He concludes, "The primary feature of well-being can be seen in terms of how a person can 'function,' taking that term in a very broad sense" (197). He restates this idea twice: "The primary feature of a person's well-being is the functioning vector that he or she achieves" (198). And, "the central feature of well-being is the ability to achieve valuable functionings" (200). The person, he concludes, must evaluate the important functionings, and his or her well-being will thus be relative to his or her valuation.

These statements already introduce a question: Is well-being the opportunity (capability) for valuable functionings, or their achievement? These initial statements appear to suggest the former. The ensuing discussion confirms this picture but complicates it by arguing that freedom is just one aspect of well-being. Achieved well-being consists centrally in achieved functionings, but the opportunity to choose them is also "relevant to assessing the well-being aspect" of a person (201). Consider two people, one fasting and one starving: Sen says that there is no difference between "the actual well-being levels achieved by the two," but there is still a difference in freedom: the person who fasts has low nutritional status out of choice, and this difference is relevant to assessing the person's well-being. It is this freedom to choose to function or not to function that Sen henceforth calls "well-being freedom," and the surrounding discussion strongly suggests that he views this freedom not as merely instrumental to well-being but as a constituent part of a person's well-being.

So for Sen, freedom—by which he seems to mean two-way freedom, freedom to do or not do—is intrinsic to well-being itself. Well-being freedom is this freedom that "concentrates on a person's capability to have various functioning vectors and to enjoy the corresponding well-being achievements" (203). Sen now contrasts this notion of freedom with one that he calls "broader," "related to the agency aspect of a person" (203). This is a bit surprising, since it would seem that agency was already being considered. Let us see how Sen states the crucial distinction:

A person's "agency freedom" refers to what the person is free to do and achieve in pursuit of whatever goals or values he or she regards as important. A person's agency aspect cannot be understood without taking note of his or her aims, objectives, allegiances, obligations, and—in a broad sense—the person's conception of the good. Whereas well-being freedom is freedom to achieve something in particular, viz., well-being, the idea of agency freedom is more general, since it is not tied to any one type of aim. Agency freedom is freedom to achieve whatever the person, as a responsible agent, decides he or she should achieve. That *open conditionality* makes the nature of agency freedom quite different from that of well-being freedom, which concentrates on a particular type of objective and judges opportunities correspondingly. (203–204)

This distinction is not puzzling to a utilitarian, for whom well-being has a narrow sense connected to happiness or desire satisfaction. But Sen has already rejected those narrow notions of well-being and has defined it in accordance with whatever a person values, that is, with that person's conception of the good. Since he here defines agency in terms of a conception of the good, the need to introduce this additional notion is altogether puzzling, suggesting that he has retreated to a narrower notion of well-being and now needs agency to do the work done (in the previous lecture) by the broad notion of well-being. How might we try to make sense of the distinction?

We might conjecture, first, that agency freedom is broader because it includes the freedom not to pursue a goal, as well as the freedom to pursue it (so one could have well-being freedom but not agency freedom, under the aegis of certain paternalistic policies that force people to do what they value, for example, to lead healthy lives, and remove the opportunity to do otherwise. Sen, however, has already made it clear that the freedom to do otherwise is an element of well-being freedom. We might then conjecture that agency freedom is broader because it includes the freedom to pursue allegiances and goals that are not connected to one's personal life and how one is doing as an individual. Sen, however, insists that agency freedom involves a person's "conception of the good" and is personal in just that sense: it involves everything a person values in aiming at the good. Is well-being freedom narrower, as initially defined? It would seem not, since the agent is invited to consider all the functionings and to value them. Sen does not associate agency freedom with the freedom to pursue things that are altogether irrelevant to a person's conception of the good—although he might have done so. Thus the freedom to pull up blades of grass all day is just as irrelevant to a person's agency freedom, according to Sen, as it is to that same person's well-being freedom, if the person attaches no importance at all to that functioning. If, by contrast, a person values pulling up blades of grass, then the opportunity to choose that functioning will be relevant to both that person's agency freedom and to her well-being freedom.

I conclude that the distinction is obscure and not useful to one who, like Sen, has rejected (on good grounds) utilitarian notions of well-being. It is a vestige of utilitarianism inside Sen's nonutilitarian project.

To compare my own notion of freedom with Sen's is complicated, since mine is a political conception and not a comprehensive conception of both well-being and agency. It thus says nothing at all about freedoms to pursue parts of people's comprehensive conceptions of the good that are not included within the political conception. The political conception certainly does value capabilities that have a large impact on people's abilities to pursue their varied conceptions of the good. Capabilities such as health, bodily integrity, practical reason, and religious liberty are on the list precisely because they are valuable in the pursuit of many different life plans. But it does not take a stand on each and every freedom to pursue each and every element in all the conceptions of the good, nor does it guarantee every citizen an opportunity to pursue every such element. Some conceptions of the good, for example, require expensive resources that would compromise the state's ability to protect its citizens in fundamental matters.

Where the political conception does take a stand, however, the capabilities are valued as freedoms to pursue a partial political conception of well-being. And I agree thoroughly with Sen's arguments favoring a capability-based conception of well-being over desire-based and mental-state conceptions—although my use of the capabilities is political rather than comprehensive. But because what is valued is the freedom to do or not to do, agency is woven throughout. As of now, I conclude that there is no need for a distinction between agency freedom and well-being freedom, if we have a sufficiently refined conception of well-being.

Chapter Notes

These notes are intended as guides for further reading. They are not necessary for the meaning of the text, but they point the reader to publications (cited in full in the Bibliography) in which various claims in the text are further defended and/or debated.

References to the list of works by Nussbaum and Sen should be self-explanatory. Section III of the Bibliography includes publications, by authors other than Nussbaum and Sen, that are directly about the Capabilities Approach. It gives a highly selective but, I hope, useful review of the literature for those who want to read further. Section IV includes all the other material referred to in the text—material germane to the issues under discussion, but not explicitly invoking or elaborating the Capabilities Approach. To save the reader from searching for a given reference in two distinct lists, I have inserted (III) or (IV) after each such reference.

Chapter 1

The Human Development Reports are published every year by the United Nations Development Programme and Oxford University Press, New York.

Vasanti's story is further discussed in Nussbaum 3, along with other related stories and data.

SEWA, and Bhatt's work, are described in Rose (IV). For the struggles of women like those in SEWA, see Bhatt (IV).

On differential nutrition and health care for girls, see Sen and Drèze 14, 16, and 18. On sex-selective abortion, see 18. See also Sen 33, 34.

On unequal property and inheritance laws, see Agarwal (IV), *A Field of One's Own*. On domestic violence and landownership, see Agarwal and Panda (III). Domestic violence is further discussed in Nussbaum 69.

For the empirical work mentioned in the final paragraph, see Wolff and De-Shalit (III).

CHAPTER 2

The most extensive discussions of these basic concepts can be found in Nussbaum 3, 6, and 55, and in Sen 7 and 9. The capabilities list presented here is the same version found in Nussbaum, 3, 6, and 55.

The idea of political liberalism is analyzed and contrasted with other types of liberalism in Larmore (IV); and Rawls (IV), *Political Liberalism*. A key issue, objectivity, is discussed in Nussbaum 46.

For discussion of capability and functioning in health policy, see Arneson (IV).

On the idea of human dignity, see Nussbaum 79 and 48; it is put to work in Nussbaum 3 and 6.

On tragic choice, see Sen 6 and Nussbaum 43. See also Richardson (III), *Practical Reasoning*.

CHAPTER 3

Criticisms of the GDP approach are developed in Nussbaum 3, 6, and 55, and in Sen 3, 5, and 9. Compare the related criticisms in Stiglitz, Sen, Fitoussi, et al. (IV).

Criticisms of utilitarian approaches are developed in Nussbaum 3, 6, 33, and 55, and in Sen 2, 4, 9, 19, 21, 23, 26, and 38. The utilitarian notion of happiness is dissected in Nussbaum 65 and 83. See also Schokkaert

(III). A very interesting attempt to defend a subtle version of comprehensive welfarism is in Posner (IV).

Internal consistency of choice is discussed in Sen 35; see also 20. A plural conception of utility is advocated in Sen 26.

Adaptive preferences are discussed in Elster (IV); in Sen 3 and 4; and in Nussbaum 3 (chapter 2).

The intrinsic importance of agency and freedom is discussed in Sen 9, See also Sen 27.

For Rawls's accounts of the primary goods, see Rawls (IV), *A Theory of Justice* and *Political Liberalism*. Sen's point about variable needs for resources was first articulated in Sen 24, and then in many subsequent books and articles: see especially Sen 3, 4, 7, 9, and 38. Nussbaum discusses this issue in 3, 6, and 55.

The relationship between capabilities and human rights is discussed in Sen 49 and in Nussbaum 3, 6, 34, 55, and 86. For related issues about rights, see Sen 27.

CHAPTER 4

For the difference between Sen's approach and mine, see Nussbaum 55; compare Sen 9.

Sen's critique of Rawls is in Sen 13.

My approach to political justification is laid out in Nussbaum 3, chapter 2, and further developed in Nussbaum 63, replying to the characterization in Okin (IV), which is inaccurate in a number of ways. Rawls's famous approach is in Rawls (IV), *A Theory of Justice*. On the process of self-education, see also Nussbaum 35.

For the notion of overlapping consensus, see Rawls (IV), *Political Liberalism;* my use of it is described in Nussbaum 6.

My critique of informed-desire welfarism is in Nussbaum 3, chapter 2. See also Harsanyi (IV); Brandt (IV); and Hampton (IV). On desire as an intelligent part of the personality, see Nussbaum 3, chapter 2. (Here I am criticizing Scanlon [IV], *What We Owe to Each Other.*)

My extensive critique of social contract views is developed in Nussbaum 6, with both historical and contemporary discussions and a sustained focus on Rawls. My critique of Rawls is discussed in a very interesting way in Richardson (III), "Rawlsian Social-Contract Theory." I reply in the same journal number.

For Scanlon's ethical contractarianism, see Scanlon (IV), *What We Owe to Each Other,* and for one attempt to develop a political theory based upon it, see Barry (IV). Scanlon (IV), "Value, Desire, and the Quality of Life," suggests that his own approach would be quite different, involving a substantive list.

On political liberalism and related concepts, see Larmore (IV); and Rawls (IV), *Political Liberalism.* My own commitment to political liberalism as the right way to frame the Capabilities Approach was first stated in Nussbaum 32, and from that time on reiterated in all major statements of the approach. It is thus simply inaccurate to describe the view as a form of "cosmopolitanism," as I explain in Nussbaum 77.

On religion and the state, see Nussbaum 8 and 76.

On the approach as "outcome-oriented" but not (comprehensively) consequentialist, see Nussbaum 6.

On emotions, see Nussbaum 4, 5, 7, 9, 23, 24, 26, 53, 73, 80, 83, and 88; see Sen 21.

CHAPTER 5

Defenses of (a culturally sensitive form of) universalism are in Nussbaum 3, chapter 1, and Nussbaum 19, 22, 25, and 27.

For Sen's critique of the idea that key concepts involved in the human rights movement are all "Western values," see Sen 42, 43, 11; Sen and Nussbaum at Nussbaum 20.

On the relationship between religion and other key political norms, including the equality of women, see Nussbaum 2, 3, 7, 8, 30, 40, 50, 64, 71, 75, 76, 78, 82, 85; Sen 12.

On Tagore, Gandhi, and Nehru, see Sen 11; Nussbaum 7, 10; Nussbaum and Doniger 15.

On protections for social and economic rights in the Indian and South African Constitutions, see Nussbaum 78.

On culture not being a monolith, see Benhabib in Nussbaum and Glover 12, and see Nussbaum 3.

On the need to articulate a system of liberty, see Richardson's interesting critique in Richardson (III), "The Social Background." I believe that this is the sort of thing I am doing in Nussbaum 8, though I was not yet aware of Richardson's views when I wrote it.

My view on humanitarian intervention is given in Nussbaum 6.

CHAPTER 6

My own arguments extending the Capabilities Approach beyond the nation are in Nussbaum 6, anticipated by Nussbaum 67. Major contributions to this area are made in Rawls (IV), *The Law of Peoples;* Beitz (IV); and Pogge (IV), *Realizing Rawls* and *World Poverty and Human Rights.* See also Unger's (IV) utilitarian view, and Singer (IV).

On fairness problems with individual philanthropy, see Murphy (IV); and, for psychological evidence that empathic emotion does not lead to fair or balanced assistance, see Batson (IV).

On the importance of giving people a personal sphere of control, see Williams (IV), and for an attractive solution, see Nagel (IV).

CHAPTER 7

On non-Western roots of these ideas, see Sen 11 and 42, and Nussbaum 7.

Aristotle's ideas as the basis for the approach are discussed in Nussbaum 18, 19, 21, 22, 25, 27. Nussbaum 78 contains a comprehensive set of textual references to the passages of Aristotle pertinent to this discussion. For his criticism of the pursuit of wealth, see *Politics,* 1256a1–1258b8. The criticism of Plato's corporate state is in *Politics,* Book II; for "the good of each," see 1261a17–b10.

For Stoic ideas of dignity and their implications, see Nussbaum 31 and 78. Some limitations are discussed in Nussbaum 37, 48, and 53.

Roger Williams is discussed in Nussbaum 8, chapter 2.

On Smith and education, see the related discussion in Nussbaum 78. On trade restrictions, see *The Wealth of Nations* (hereafter WN), 452–498. An excellent discussion of Smith's defense of government activity to limit the disproportionate influence of financial interests is in Rothschild (IV). On the "tender plant," see WN 97. On education, see WN 782–788.

For analysis of ideas of capability in Paine's *Rights of Man,* see Nussbaum 78.

See Barker (IV); Green (IV); on the relationship of Green's ideas to British political developments, see Harris and Morrow (IV), "Introduction," and Deigh (IV). For similar ideas in the New Deal, see Sunstein (IV).

CHAPTER 8

For disadvantage, see Wolff and De-Shalit (III).

For gender and human capabilities, see Nussbaum 2, 3, 12, 25, 26, 35, 39, 54, 55, 56, 62, 63, 69, and 71; Sen 32, 33, 34, 40, 47, and 48; Agarwal and Panda (III); Agarwwal, Humphries, and Robeyns, eds. (III).

For related philosophical work, see Nussbaum 2, 5, 28, 29, 30, 38, 40, 41, 44, 50, 51, 52, 57, 58, 59, 66, and 68.

On the objectification of women on the Internet, see the essays in Levmore and Nussbaum 16.

On sexual orientation, see Nussbaum 2, 5, and 9. See also Ball (III).

Disability and care are the central issues in Nussbaum 6, with extensive discussion of the views of other theorists. New claims about the political rights of people with cognitive disabilities, going beyond Nussbaum 6, are in Nussbaum 87, in a journal issue devoted to this topic that contains a lot of pertinent material by others. For an excellent critique, see Richardson (III), "Rawlsian Social-Contract Theory." *Human Development Report* 1999 focuses on the issue of care and care labor.

For Nussbaum's writings on education, see 1, 10, 17, 59, 72, 74, and 81. Legal and constitutional issues relating to education are discussed in 78 and 68. (The cases mentioned here are further analyzed in 78.)

For the findings of the Pratichi Trust, see *The Pratichi Education Report* (IV).

The cases referred to are, from India: *Mohini Jain v. State of Karnataka,* AIR 1992 1858; *Unnikrishnan J. P. v. State of Andhra Pradesh,* AIR 1993 SC 2178. From the United States: *Plyler v. Doe,* 457 U.S. 202 (1982).

For Nussbaum's views on animal rights, see Nussbaum 6, 88, and 89, and see Korsgaard (IV); Bendik-Keymer (III).

For environmental quality see Holland (III), "Ecology and the Limits of Justice," and "Justice and the Environment in Nussbaum's 'Capabilities Approach'"; Bendik-Keymer (III). For Sen on population, see 39 and 41.

On capabilities and constitutions, see Nussbaum 78; on the task of government, see Nussbaum 6 and 78. For Sen's denial of a conceptual connection between capabilities and government, see Sen 49. The issue of religious free exercise is extensively discussed in Nussbaum 8, where all the court cases mentioned here are analyzed, and also in 76 and 78.

For Sen and public debate, see 11, 12, and 13.

The Free Exercise cases mentioned are:

Sherbert v. Verner, 374 U.S. 398 (1963)

Employment Division v. Smith, 494 U.S. 872 (1990) (the case that brought about a large change in the framework of interpretation)

People v. Philips, N.Y. Court of General Sessions, June 14, 1813 (this case, involving the priest and the confessional, was privately recorded and reprinted in the religion casebook edited by McConnell, Garvey, and Berg, pp. 103–109)

Swann v. Pack, 527 S.W. 2d 99 (Tenn. 1974) (the case involving snake handling)

For my prior work on emotions, see Nussbaum 4, 5, 23, 24, 26, and 32. For work that will ultimately form a part of the new project in progress, see 53, 75, 80, 85, and 90.

Bibliography

I. Works by Martha Nussbaum

This list is highly selective and includes only works relevant to chapter discussions.

Books

1. *Cultivating Humanity: A Classical Defense of Reform in Liberal Education.* Cambridge, MA: Harvard University Press, 1997.
2. *Sex and Social Justice.* Oxford: Oxford University Press, 1999.
3. *Women and Human Development: The Capabilities Approach.* New York: Cambridge University Press, 2000.
4. *Upheavals of Thought: The Intelligence of Emotions.* Cambridge: Cambridge University Press, 2001.
5. *Hiding from Humanity: Disgust, Shame, and the Law.* Princeton: Princeton University Press, 2004.
6. *Frontiers of Justice: Disability, Nationality, Species Membership.* Cambridge, MA: Harvard University Press, 2006.
7. *The Clash Within: Democracy, Religious Violence, and India's Future.* Cambridge, MA: Harvard University Press, 2007.
8. *Liberty of Conscience: In Defense of America's Tradition of Religious Equality.* New York: Basic Books, 2008.
9. *From Disgust to Humanity: Sexual Orientation and Constitutional Law.* New York: Oxford University Press, 2010.

10. *Not For Profit: Why Democracy Needs the Humanities*. Princeton: Princeton University Press, 2010.

Edited Books

11. (with Amartya Sen) *The Quality of Life*. Oxford: Clarendon Press, 1993.
12. (with Jonathan Glover) *Women, Culture, and Development*. Oxford: Clarendon Press, 1995.
13. (with Joshua Cohen) *Is Multiculturalism Good for Women?* Princeton: Princeton University Press, 1999.
14. (with Cass Sunstein) *Animal Rights: Current Debates, New Directions*. New York: Oxford University Press, 2004.
15. (with Wendy Doniger) *India: Implementing Pluralism and Democracy*. New York: Oxford University Press, forthcoming.
16. (with Saul Levmore) *The Offensive Internet: Speech, Privacy, and Reputation*. Cambridge, MA: Harvard University Press, forthcoming.
17. (with Zoya Hasan) *Affirmative Action in Higher Education* (tentative title), in preparation.

Articles

18. "Nature, Function, and Capability: Aristotle on Political Distribution." In *Oxford Studies in Ancient Philosophy*, supp. vol. l, 145–184. New York: Oxford University Press, 1988. Reprinted in *Marx and Aristotle*, ed. G. McCarthy, 175–212. Savage, MD: Rowman and Littlefield, 1992.
19. "Non-Relative Virtues: An Aristotelian Approach." *Midwest Studies in Philosophy* 13 (1988): 32–53. Expanded version in Nussbaum and Sen, *The Quality of Life*, 242–269.
20. (with Amartya Sen) "Internal Criticism and Indian Rationalist Traditions." In *Relativism: Interpretation and Confrontation*, ed. M. Krausz, 299–325. Notre Dame, IN: University of Notre Dame Press, 1989.
21. "Aristotelian Social Democracy." In *Liberalism and the Good*, ed. R. B. Douglass, G. Mara, and H. Richardson, 203–252. New York: Routledge, 1990. Reprinted in *Aristotle and Modern Politics*, ed. A. Tessi-

tore, 47–104. Notre Dame, IN: University of Notre Dame Press, 2002.

22. "Human Functioning and Social Justice: In Defense of Aristotelian Essentialism." *Political Theory* 20 (1992): 202–246. Shorter version published as "Social Justice and Universalism: In Defense of an Aristotelian Account of Human Functioning." *Modern Philology* 90 (1993): supp., S46-S73. German version published as "Menschliches Handeln und soziale Gerechtigkeit." In *Gemeinschaft und Gerechtigkeit*, ed. H. Brunkhorst and M. Brumlik. Frankfurt: Fischer Taschenbuch, 1993.

23. "Tragedy and Self-Sufficiency: Plato and Aristotle on Fear and Pity." In *Oxford Studies in Ancient Philosophy* 10 (1992): 107–160. A shorter version is in *Essays on Aristotle's Poetics*, ed. A. Rorty, 261–290. Princeton: Princeton University Press, 1992.

24. "Equity and Mercy." *Philosophy and Public Affairs* 22 (1993): 83–125. Reprinted in *Punishment: A Philosophy and Public Affairs Reader*, ed. A. John Simmons et al., 145–187. Princeton University Press, 1995. Also reprinted in *Punishment and Rehabilitation*, ed. Jeffrie Murphy, 212–248. Belmont, CA: Wadsworth, 1995; and in *Literature and Legal Problem Solving*, ed. Paul Heald, 15–54. Durham, N.C.: Carolina Academic Press, 1998.

25. "Human Capabilities, Female Human Beings." In Nussbaum and Glover, *Women, Culture, and Development*, 61–104.

26. "Emotions and Women's Capabilities." In Nussbaum and Glover, *Women, Culture, and Development*, 360–395.

27. "Aristotle on Human Nature and the Foundations of Ethics." In *World, Mind, and Ethics: Essays on the Philosophy of Bernard Williams*, ed. J. E. G. Altham and Ross Harrison, 86–131. Cambridge: Cambridge University Press, 1995.

28. "Objectification." *Philosophy and Public Affairs* 24 (1995): 249–291. Reprinted in *The Philosophy of Sex*, ed. Alan Soble, 3rd ed. Lanham, MD: Rowman and Littlefield, 1997. (Also in Nussbaum, *Sex and Social Justice*.)

29. "The Feminist Critique of Liberalism." In *Women's Voices, Women's*

Rights: Oxford Amnesty Lectures 1996, ed. Alison Jeffries. Boulder, CO: Westview, 1999. Also published in pamphlet form as the Lindley Lecture for 1997, University of Kansas Press. (Also in Nussbaum, *Sex and Social Justice.*)

30. "Religion and Women's Human Rights." In *Religion and Contemporary Liberalism,* ed. Paul Weithman, 93–137. Notre Dame, IN: Notre Dame University Press, 1997. (Also in Nussbaum, *Sex and Social Justice.*)

31. "Kant and Stoic Cosmopolitanism." *Journal of Political Philosophy* 5 (1997): 1–25. Also as "Kant und stoisches Weltbürgertum." In *Frieden durch Recht: Kants Friedensidee und das Problem einer neuen Weltordnung,* ed. Matthias Lutz-Bachmann and James Bohman, 45–75. Frankfurt: Suhrkamp, 1996. Also in *Perpetual Peace,* ed. James Bohman and Matthias Lutz-Bachmann, 25–58. Cambridge, MA: MIT Press, 1997.

32. "The Good as Discipline, the Good as Freedom." In *Ethics of Consumption: The Good Life, Justice, and Global Stewardship,* ed. David A. Crocker and Toby Linden, 312–341. Lanham, MD: Rowman and Littlefield, 1998.

33. "Flawed Foundations: The Philosophical Critique of (a particular type of) Economics." *University of Chicago Law Review* 64 (1997): 1197–1214.

34. "Capabilities and Human Rights." *Fordham Law Review* 66 (1997): 273–300. A revised version is in *Global Justice, Transnational Politics,* ed. Pablo De Greiff and Ciaran Cronin, 117–150. Cambridge, MA: MIT Press, 2002.

35. "Public Philosophy and International Feminism." *Ethics* 108 (1998): 762–796.

36. "Virtue Ethics: A Misleading Category?" *Journal of Ethics* 3 (1999): 163–201.

37. "Duties of Justice, Duties of Material Aid: Cicero's Problematic Legacy." *Journal of Political Philosophy* 7 (1999): 1–31. Revised version in *Stoicism: Traditions and Transformations,* ed. S. Strange and J. Zupko, 214–249. Cambridge: Cambridge University Press, 2004.

38. "A Plea for Difficulty." In *Is Multiculturalism Bad for Women?* ed. J. Cohen, M. Howard, and M. Nussbaum, 105–114. Princeton: Princeton University Press, 1999.

39. "Women and Equality: The Capabilities Approach." *International Labour Review* 138 (1999): 227–245. Reprinted in *Women, Gender and Work*, ed. Martha Fetherolf Loutfi, 45–68. Geneva: International Labour Office, 2001.

40. "Religion and Women's Equality: The Case of India." In *Obligations of Citizenship and Demands of Faith*, ed. Nancy Rosenblum, 335–402. Princeton: Princeton University Press, 2000.

41. "Is Privacy Bad for Women? What the Indian Constitutional Tradition Can Teach Us about Sex Equality." *The Boston Review* 25 (April/May 2000): 42–47.

42. "Aristotle, Politics, and Human Capabilities: A Response to Antony, Arneson, Charlesworth, and Mulgan." *Ethics* 111 (2000): 102–140.

43. "The Costs of Tragedy: Some Moral Limits of Cost-Benefit Analysis." *Journal of Legal Studies* 29 (2000): 1005–1036. Reprinted in *Cost-Benefit Analysis: Legal, Economic and Philosophical Perspectives*, ed. Matthew D. Adler and Eric A. Posner, 169–200. Chicago: University of Chicago Press, 2000.

44. "The Future of Feminist Liberalism." Presidential Address delivered to the Central Division of the American Philosophical Association, *Proceedings and Addresses of the American Philosophical Association* 74 (2000): 47–79. Reprinted in *The Subject of Care: Feminist Perspectives on Dependency*, ed. Eva Kittay and Ellen K. Feder, 186–214. Lanham, MD: Rowman and Littlefield, 2002. Also reprinted in *Setting the Moral Compass: Essays by Women Philosophers*, ed. Cheshire Calhoun, 72–90. New York: Oxford University Press, 2004.

45. "India: Implementing Sex Equality through Law." *Chicago Journal of International Law* 2 (2001): 35–58.

46. "Political Objectivity." *New Literary History* 32 (2001): 883–906.

47. "Sex, Laws, and Inequality: What India Can Teach the United States." *Daedalus*, Winter 2002, 95–106.

48. "The Worth of Human Dignity: Two Tensions in Stoic Cosmopoli-

tanism." In *Philosophy and Power in the Graeco-Roman World: Essays in Honour of Miriam Griffin,* ed. G. Clark and T. Rajak, 31–49. Oxford: Clarendon Press, 2002.

49. "Aristotelische Sozialdemokratie: Die Verteidigung universaler Werte in einer pluralistischen Welt." In *Für eine aristotelische Sozialdemokratie,* ed. Julian Nida-Rümelin and Wolfgang Thierse, 17–40. A publication of the Kulturforum of the SDP. Essen: Klartext Verlag, 2002. Reprinted as "Aristotelian Social Democracy: Defending Universal Values in a Pluralistic World." *Internationale Zeitschrift für Philosophie* (2003): 115–129.

50. "Rawls and Feminism." In *The Cambridge Companion to Rawls,* ed. Samuel Freeman, 488–520. Cambridge: Cambridge University Press, 2003. Spanish translation in *Estudos Públicos* 103 (2006): 359–394.

51. "Women and the Law of Peoples." Symposium on John Rawls's *The Law of Peoples: Politics, Philosophy, and Economics* 1 (2002): 283–306.

52. "Sex Equality, Liberty, and Privacy: A Comparative Approach to the Feminist Critique." In *India's Living Constitution: Ideas, Practices, Controversies,* ed. E. Sridharan, Z. Hasan, and R. Sudarshan, 242–283. New Delhi: Permanent Black, 2002. A shortened version is published under the title "What's Privacy Got to Do with It? A Comparative Approach to the Feminist Critique." In *Women and the United States Constitution: History, Interpretation, Practice,* ed. Sibyl A. Schwarzenbach and Patricia Smith, 153–175. New York: Columbia University Press, 2003.

53. "Compassion and Terror." *Daedalus,* Winter 2003, 10–26. A slightly different version, same title, is in *Terrorism and International Justice,* ed. James Sterba, 229–252. New York: Oxford University Press, 2003.

54. "Women's Capabilities and Social Justice." In *Gender Justice, Development, and Rights,* ed. Maxine Molyneux and Shahra Razavi, 45–77. Oxford: Oxford University Press, 2002.

55. "Capabilities as Fundamental Entitlements: Sen and Social Justice." *Feminist Economics* 9 (2003): 33–59. Reprinted in *Amartya Sen's Work*

and Ideas: A Gender Perspective, ed. Bina Agarwal, Jane Humphries, and Ingrid Robeyns, 35–62. Oxford: Routledge, 2005. Also reprinted in India in *Capabilities, Freedom, and Equality: Amartya Sen's Work from a Gender Perspective,* same editors, 39–69. Delhi: Oxford University Press, 2006. A related shorter version is published as "Poverty and Human Functioning: Capabilities as Fundamental Entitlements." In *Poverty and Inequality,* ed. David B. Grusky and Ravi Kanbur, 47–75. Stanford, CA: Stanford University Press, 2006. A related longer version is published as "Constitutions and Capabilities." In *Democracy in a Global World,* ed. Deen K. Chatterjee, 111–144. Lanham, MD: Rowman and Littlefield, 2008. Reprinted in *The Global Justice Reader,* ed. Thom Brooks, 598–614. Malden, MA: Blackwell, 2008.

56. "Promoting Women's Capabilities." In *Global Tensions,* ed. Lourdes Benaria and Savitri Bisnath, 241–256. New York: Routledge, 2004.

57. "The Modesty of Mrs. Bajaj: India's Problematic Route to Sexual Harassment Law." In *Directions in Sexual Harassment Law,* ed. Catharine A. MacKinnon and Reva B. Siegel, 633–671. New Haven: Yale University Press, 2004.

58. "Gender and Governance: An Introduction." In *Essays on Gender and Governance,* ed. Martha Nussbaum, Amrita Basu, Yasmin Tambiah, and Niraja Gopal Jayal, 1–19. New Delhi: United Nations Development Programme Resource Centre, 2003.

59. "Women's Education: A Global Challenge." *Signs* 29 (2004): 325–355. Reprinted in *Women and Citizenship,* ed. Marilyn Friedman, 188–213. New York: Oxford University Press, 2005.

60. "Capabilities and Disabilities: Justice for Mentally Disabled Citizens." *Philosophical Topics* 30 (2002): 133–165.

61. "Beyond 'Compassion and Humanity': Justice for Non-Human Animals." In *Animal Rights: Current Debates and New Directions,* ed. Cass R. Sunstein and Martha C. Nussbaum, 299–320. New York: Oxford University Press, 2004.

62. "Women and Theories of Global Justice: Our Need for New Para-

digms." In *The Ethics of Assistance: Morality and the Distant Needy*, ed. Deen Chatterjee, 147–176. Cambridge: Cambridge University Press, 2004.

63. "On Hearing Women's Voices: A Reply to Susan Okin." *Philosophy and Public Affairs* 32 (2004): 193–205.

64. "'On Equal Condition': Constitutions as Protectors of the Vulnerable." In *Will Secular India Survive?* ed. Mushirul Hasan and Hasan Saroor, 22–49. New Delhi: ImprintOne, 2004.

65. "Mill between Bentham and Aristotle." *Daedalus*, Spring 2004, 60–68. Reprinted in *Economics and Happiness*, ed. Luigino Bruni and Pier Luigi Porta, 170–183. Oxford: Oxford University Press, 2005.

66. "Body of the Nation: Why Women Were Mutilated in Gujarat." *The Boston Review* 29 (2004): 33–38. A slightly different version published as "Rape and Murder in Gujarat: Violence against Muslim Women in the Struggle for Hindu Supremacy." In *'Holy War' and Gender, 'Gotteskrieg' und Geschlecht*, ed. Christina von Braun, Ulrike Brunotte, Gabriele Dietze, Daniela Hrzán, Gabriele Jähnert, and Dagmar Pruin, 121–142. *Berliner Gender Studies*, vol. 2. Münster: Transaction, 2006.

67. "Beyond the Social Contract: Toward Global Justice." *The Tanner Lectures on Human Values* 24: 413–508. Salt Lake City: University of Utah Press, 2004.

68. "India, Sex Equality, and Constitutional Law." In *Constituting Women: The Gender of Constitutional Jurisprudence*, ed. Beverly Baines and Ruth Rubio-Marin, 174–204. Cambridge: Cambridge University Press, 2004.

69. "Women's Bodies: Violence, Security, Capabilities." *Journal of Human Development* 6 (2005): 167–183.

70. "Wellbeing, Contracts and Capabilities." In *Rethinking Wellbeing*, ed. Lenore Manderson, 27–44. Perth, Australia: API Network, 2005.

71. "Religion, Culture, and Sex Equality" (paper overlapping with chapter 3 of *Women and Human Development*, published after delay of some years). In *Men's Laws, Women's Lives: A Constitutional Perspective*

on Religion, Common Law and Culture in South Asia, ed. Indira Jaising, 109–137. Delhi: Women Unlimited, 2005.

72. "Education and Democratic Citizenship: Beyond the Textbook Controversy." In *Islam and the Modern Age* (New Delhi) 35 (2005): 69–89. A slightly different version is published as "Freedom from Dead Habit." *The Little Magazine* (New Delhi) 6 (2005): 18–32.

73. "The Comic Soul: Or, This Phallus that Is Not One." In *The Soul of Tragedy: Essays on Athenian Drama,* ed. Victoria Pedrick and Steven M. Oberhelman, 155–180. Chicago: University of Chicago Press, 2005.

74. "Education and Democratic Citizenship: Capabilities and Quality Education." *Journal of Human Development* 7 (2006): 385–395.

75. "Radical Evil in the Lockean State: The Neglect of the Political Emotions." *Journal of Moral Philosophy* 3 (2006): 159–178. A longer version is "Radical Evil in Liberal Democracies." In *Democracy and the New Religious Pluralism,* ed. Thomas Banchoff, 171–202. New York: Oxford University Press, 2007.

76. "Liberty of Conscience: The Attack on Equal Respect." *Journal of Human Development* 8 (2007): 337–358.

77. "The Capabilities Approach and Ethical Cosmopolitanism: A Response to Noah Feldman." *Yale Law Journal: The Pocket Part,* October 30, 2007, http://thepocketpart.org/2007/10/30/nussbaum.html.

78. "Constitutions and Capabilities: 'Perception' against Lofty Formalism." Supreme Court Foreword, *Harvard Law Review* 121 (2007): 4–97.

79. "Human Dignity and Political Entitlements." In *Human Dignity and Bioethics: Essays Commissioned by the President's Council on Bioethics,* 351–380. Washington, D.C.: President's Council on Bioethics, 2008.

80. "Toward a Globally Sensitive Patriotism." *Daedalus,* Summer 2008, 78–93.

81. "Education for Profit, Education for Freedom." Special lecture 1, Institute for Development Studies Kolkata, printed as pamphlet, March 2008.

82. "The Clash Within: Democracy and the Hindu Right." In *Arguments for a Better World: Essays in Honor of Amartya Sen,* ed. Kaushik Basu and Ravi Kanbur, vol. 2, 503–521. Oxford: Oxford University Press, 2008. Also published in a slightly different form in *Journal of Human Development* 9 (2008): 357–376.

83. "Who Is the Happy Warrior: Philosophy Poses Questions to Psychology." *Journal of Legal Studies* 37 (2008): 81–114. Reprinted in *Law and Happiness,* ed. Eric A. Posner and Cass R. Sunstein, 81–114. Chicago: University of Chicago Press, 2010.

84. "Land of My Dreams: Islamic Liberalism under Fire in India." *The Boston Review* 34 (2009): 10–14. Reprinted in *The Idea of a University: Jamia Millia Islamia,* ed. Rakhshanda Jalil, 13–28. New Delhi: Aakar, 2009.

85. "Nationalism and Development: Can There Be a Decent Patriotism?" *Indian Journal of Human Development* 2 (2008): 259–278.

86. "Capabilities, Entitlements, Rights: Supplementation and Critique." *Journal of Human Development and Capabilities,* forthcoming.

87. "The Capabilities of People with Cognitive Disabilities." *Metaphilosophy* 40 (2009): 331–351. Reprinted in *Cognitive Disability and Its Challenge to Moral Philosophy,* ed. Eva Kittay and Licia Carlson. Wiley-Blackwell, 2010.

88. "Compassion: Human and Animal." In *Ethics and Humanity: Themes from the Philosophy of Jonathan Glover,* ed. N. Ann Davis, Richard Keshen, and Jeff McMahan, 202–226. New York: Oxford University Press, 2010.

89. "The Capabilities Approach and Animal Entitlements." In *Handbook on Ethics and Animals,* ed. Tom Beauchamp. Oxford: Oxford University Press, forthcoming.

90. "Equality and Love at the End of *The Marriage of Figaro:* Forging Democratic Emotions." *Journal of Human Development and Capabilities* 11 (2010): 397–423.

91. "Abortion, Dignity, and a Capabilities Approach" (with Rosalind

Dixon). In *Feminist Constitutionalism,* ed. Beverly Baines, Daphne Barak-Erez, and Tsvi Kahana. Cambridge: Cambridge University Press, forthcoming.

II. WORKS BY AMARTYA SEN

The following works represent a small selection of Sen's relevant writings

Books

1. *Poverty and Famines: An Essay on Entitlement and Deprivation.* Oxford: Clarendon Press, 1981.
2. *Choice, Welfare, and Measurement.* Oxford: Clarendon Press, 1982.
3. *Resources, Values, and Development.* Cambridge, MA: Harvard University Press, 1984.
4. *Commodities and Capabilities.* Amsterdam: North-Holland, 1985.
5. *The Standard of Living.* Tanner Lectures, 1985, ed. G. Hawthorn, with discussion by others. Cambridge University Press, 1987.
6. *On Ethics and Economics.* Oxford: Blackwell, 1987.
7. *Inequality Reexamined.* New York and Cambridge, MA: Russell Sage and Harvard University Press, 1992.
8. *On Economic Inequality,* expanded ed. Oxford: Clarendon Press, 1996. Originally published in 1973 by Oxford University Press.
9. *Development as Freedom.* New York: Knopf, 1999.
10. *Rationality and Freedom.* Cambridge, MA: Harvard University Press, 2002.
11. *The Argumentative Indian.* London: Allen Lane, 2005.
12. *Identity and Violence: The Illusion of Destiny.* New York: W. W. Norton, 2006.
13. *The Idea of Justice.* Cambridge, MA: Harvard University Press, 2009.

With Jean Drèze:

14. *Hunger and Public Action.* Oxford: Clarendon Press, 1989.

15. (eds.) *The Political Economy of Hunger,* 3 vols. Oxford: Clarendon Press, 1990.
16. *India: Economic Development and Social Opportunity.* Oxford and Delhi: Oxford University Press, 1995.
17. (eds.) *Indian Development: Selected Regional Perspectives.* Oxford and Delhi: Oxford University Press, 1996.
18. *India: Development and Participation.* Oxford and Delhi: Oxford University Press, 2002. (A new edition of Sen 16, but with much added material.)

With Bernard Williams:
19. (eds.) *Utilitarianism and Beyond.* Cambridge: Cambridge University Press, 1982.

Articles
20. "Behaviour and the Concept of a Preference." *Economica* 40 (1973): 241–259. (Also in Sen 2.)
21. "Rational Fools: A Critique of the Behavioural Foundations of Economic Theory." *Philosophy and Public Affairs* 6 (1977): 317–344. Widely anthologized. (Also in Sen 2.)
22. "Poverty: An Ordinal Approach to Measurement." *Econometrica* 44 (1976): 219–231. (Also in Sen 2.)
23. "Utilitarianism and Welfarism." *Journal of Philosophy* 76 (1979): 463–489.
24. "Equality of What?" In *Tanner Lectures on Human Values,* ed. S. McMurrin. Salt Lake City: University of Utah Press, 1980. (Also in Sen 2.)
25. "Description as Choice." *Oxford Economic Papers* 32 (1980): 353–369. (Also in Sen 2.)
26. "Plural Utility." *Proceedings of the Aristotelian Society* 81 (1980–1981): 193–215.
27. "Rights and Agency." *Philosophy and Public Affairs* 11 (1982): 3–39.
28. "Development: Which Way Now?" *The Economic Journal* 93 (1983): 745–762. (Also in Sen 3.)

29. "Poor, Relatively Speaking." *Oxford Economic Papers* 35 (1983): 153–169. (Also in Sen 3.)

30. "Well-Being, Agency, and Freedom: The Dewey Lectures 1984." *Journal of Philosophy* 82 (1985): 169–221.

31. "The Moral Standing of the Market." *Social Philosophy and Policy* 2 (1985): 1–19.

32. "Women's Survival as a Development Problem." *Bulletin of the American Academy of Arts and Sciences* 43 (1989).

33. "More than 100 Million Women are Missing." *New York Review of Books,* December 20, 1990.

34. "Gender and Cooperative Conflicts." In *Persistent Inequalities,* ed. Irene Tinker. New York: Oxford University Press, 1990.

35. "Internal Consistency of Choice." *Econometrica* 61 (1993): 495–521. (Also in Sen 10.)

36. "Positional Objectivity." *Philosophy and Public Affairs* 22 (1993): 126–145. (Also in Sen 10.)

37. "Markets and Freedoms." *Oxford Economic Papers* 45 (1993): 519–541. (Also in Sen 10.)

38. "Capability and Well-being." In Nussbaum and Sen, *The Quality of Life.*

39. "Population: Delusion and Reality." *New York Review of Books* September 22, 1994.

40. "Gender Inequality and Theories of Justice." In Nussbaum and Glover, *Women, Culture, and Development,* 259–273.

41. "Fertility and Coercion." *University of Chicago Law Review* 63 (1996): 1035–1051.

42. "Human Rights and Asian Values." *The New Republic,* July 14/21, 1997, 33–40.

43. "Indian Traditions and the Western Imagination." *Daedalus,* Spring 1997, 1–26.

44. "The Possibility of Social Choice." Nobel Lecture, *American Economic Review* 89 (1999), 349–378.

45. "The Discipline of Cost-Benefit Analysis." *Journal of Legal Studies* 29

(2000): 931–953. Reprinted in *Cost-Benefit Analysis,* ed. Matthew Adler and Eric Posner. Chicago: University of Chicago Press, 2000.

46. "Consequential Evaluation and Practical Reason." *Journal of Philosophy* 97 (2000): 477–502.

47. "Population and Gender Equity." *The Nation,* July 24, 2000.

48. "The Many Faces of Misogyny." *The New Republic,* September 17, 2001, 35–40.

49. "Elements of a Theory of Human Rights." *Philosophy and Public Affairs* 32 (2004): 315–356.

50. "What Do We Want from a Theory of Justice?" *Journal of Philosophy* 103 (2006): 215–238.

51. "The Place of Capability in a Theory of Justice." In Brighouse and Robeyns, eds. (III), 239–253.

III.   OTHER WORKS DEALING WITH THE CAPABILITIES APPROACH

Note that many other pertinent articles are in the edited volumes listed under Sen and Nussbaum. The plenary addresses from the annual meetings of the Human Development and Capability Association, and a selection of the submitted papers, are published in the *Journal of Human Development and Capabilities* (until 2008, called the *Journal of Human Development*). Although I'll mention a few of these, I won't try to be exhaustive. Volume 9 (2008) contains a useful bibliography of the Capabilities Approach for 2007–2008, as does vol. 10 for the following year.

Agarwal, Bina, and Pradip Panda. "Toward Freedom from Domestic Violence: The Neglected Obvious." *Journal of Human Development* 8 (2007): 359–388.

Agarwal, Bina, Jane Humphries, and Ingrid Robeyns, eds. *Amartya Sen's Work and Ideas: A Gender Perspective.* Oxford: Routledge, 2005. Published in India as *Capabilities, Freedom, and Equality: Amartya Sen's Work from a Gender Perspective.* Delhi: Oxford University Press, 2006. (Originally published as two special issues of *Feminist Economics,* 2003.)

Alkire, Sabina. *Valuing Freedoms: Sen's Capability Approach and Poverty Re-duction.* Oxford: Oxford University Press, 2002.

———. "Measuring Freedoms Alongside Well-Being." In *Well-Being in Developing Countries: New Approaches and Research Strategies,* ed. I. Gough and J. Allister McGregor. Cambridge: Cambridge University Press, 2007.

Ball, Carlos. *The Morality of Gay Rights.* New York: Routledge, 2003.

Basu, Kaushik, and Ravi Kanbur, eds. *Arguments for a Better World: Essays in Honor of Amartya Sen.* Oxford and Delhi: Oxford University Press, 2009.

Basu, Kaushik, Prasanta Pattanaik, and Kotaro Suzumura, eds. *Choice, Welfare, and Development: A Festschrift in Honor of Amartya K. Sen.* Oxford: Oxford University Press, 1995.

Bendik-Keymer, Jeremy. "From Humans to All of Life: Nussbaum's Transformation of Dignity." In *Capabilities, Gender, Equality: Toward Fundamental Entitlements,* ed. F. Comim. New York: Cambridge University Press, forthcoming.

Brighouse, Harry, and Ingrid Robeyns, eds. *Measuring Justice: Primary Goods and Capabilities.* Cambridge: Cambridge University Press, 2010.

Chiappero-Martinetti, Enrica, ed. *Debating Global Society: Reach and Limits of the Capability Approach.* Milan: Fondazione Giangiacomo Feltrinelli, 2009.

Comim, Flavio, ed. *Capabilities, Gender, Equality: Toward Fundamental Entitlements.* New York and Cambridge: Cambridge University Press, forthcoming.

Comim, Flavio, Mozaffar Qizilbash, and Sabina Alkire, eds. *The Capability Approach: Concepts, Measures and Applications.* Cambridge: Cambridge University Press, 2008.

Crocker, David A. "Functioning and Capability: The Foundations of Sen's and Nussbaum's Development Ethic." *Political Theory* 20 (1992): 584–612.

———. "Functioning and Capability: The Foundations of Sen's and Nussbaum's Development Ethic, Part 2." In Nussbaum and Glover, *Women, Culture, and Development.*

——. *Ethics of Global Development: Agency, Capability, and Deliberative Democracy.* Cambridge: Cambridge University Press, 2008.

Crocker, David A., and Ingrid Robeyns. "Capability and Agency." In *Amartya Sen,* ed. C. Morris, 60–90. Cambridge: Cambridge University Press, 2009.

Deneulin, Séverine, and Lila Shahani, eds. *An Introduction to the Human Development and Capability Approach: Freedom and Agency.* London: Earthscan/IDRC, 2009.

Drydyk, Jay. "Responsible Pluralism, Capabilities, and Human Rights." *Journal of Human Development and Capability* 12, forthcoming.

Drydyk, Jay, with Peter Penz and Pablo Bose. *Displacement by Development: Ethics and Responsibilities.* Cambridge: Cambridge University Press, 2010.

DuBois, Jean-Luc, et al., eds. *Repenser l'action collective: une approche par les capabilités.* Paris: Réseau IMPACT, 2008.

Esquith, Stephen L., and Fred Gifford, eds. *Capabilities, Power, and Institutions.* University Park, PA: Penn State Press, 2010.

Fukuda-Parr, Sakiko, and A. K. Shiva Kumar, eds. *Readings in Human Development.* Oxford: Oxford University Press, 2003.

Holland, Breena. "Ecology and the Limits of Justice: Establishing Capability Ceilings in Nussbaum's Capability Approach." *Journal of Human Development* 9 (2008): 401–426.

——. "Justice and the Environment in Nussbaum's 'Capabilities Approach': Why Sustainable Ecological Capacity Is a Meta-Capability." *Political Research Quarterly* 61 (2008): 319–332.

Jayal, Niraja Gopal. "The Challenge of Human Development: Inclusion or Democratic Citizenship?" *Journal of Human Development and Capabilities* 10 (2009): 359–374.

Kanbur, Ravi, and Kaushik Basu, eds. *Arguments for a Better World: Essays in Honor of Amartya Sen.* Oxford: Oxford University Press, 2009.

Morris, Christopher, ed. *Amartya Sen.* Contemporary Philosophy in Focus. Cambridge: Cambridge University Press, forthcoming.

Pogge, Thomas. "A Critique of the Capability Approach." In Brighouse and Robeyns, eds. (III), 17–60.

Putnam, Hilary. "Capabilities and Two Ethical Theories." *Journal of Human Development* 9 (2008): 377–388.

Qizilbash, Mozaffar. "Social Choice and Individual Capabilities." *Politics, Philosophy and Economics* 6 (2007): 169–192.

Richardson, Henry. *Practical Reasoning about Final Ends.* Cambridge: Cambridge University Press, 1997.

——. "Some Limitations of Nussbaum's Capacities." *Quinnipiac Law Review* 19 (2000): 309–332.

——. "The Stupidity of the Cost-Benefit Standard." *Journal of Legal Studies* 29 (2000): 971–1003. Reprinted in *Cost-Benefit Analysis,* ed. Matthew Adler and Eric Posner. Chicago: University of Chicago Press, 2000.

——. "Rawlsian Social-Contract Theory and the Severely Disabled." *Journal of Ethics* 10 (2006): 419–462.

——. "The Social Background of Capabilities for Freedoms." *Journal of Human Development* 8 (2007): 389–414.

Robeyns, Ingrid. "The Capability Approach: A Theoretical Survey." *Journal of Human Development* 6 (2005): 93–114.

——. "The Capability Approach in Practice." *Journal of Political Philosophy* 14 (2006): 351–376.

——. "Justice as Fairness and the Capability Approach." In Kanbur and Basu, *Arguments for a Better World,* 2009.

Schokkaert, Erik. "Capabilities and Satisfaction with Life." *Journal of Human Development* 8 (2007): 415–430.

Stewart, Frances. "*Frontiers of Justice: Disability, Nationality, Species Membership,* by Martha C. Nussbaum." *Journal of Human Development and Capabilities* 10 (2009): 153–155.

Wolff, Jonathan, and Avner De-Shalit. *Disadvantage.* New York: Oxford University Press, 2007.

IV.   OTHER WORKS CITED

Agarwal, Bina. *A Field of One's Own: Gender and Land Rights in South Asia.* Cambridge: Cambridge University Press, 1994.

——. "'Bargaining' and Gender Relations: Within and Beyond the Household." *Feminist Economics* 3 (1997): 1–51.

Arneson, Richard J. "Perfectionism and Politics." *Ethics* 111 (2000): 37–63.

Barclay, Linda. "What Kind of a Liberal Is Martha Nussbaum?" *SATS: Nordic Journal of Philosophy* 4 (2003): 5–24.

Barker, Ernest. *The Political Thought of Plato and Aristotle.* London: Dover, 1959. First published 1906 by G. P. Putnam's Sons.

Barry, Brian. *Justice as Impartiality.* Oxford: Clarendon Press, 1995.

Batson, C. Daniel. *The Altruism Question: Toward a Social-Psychological Answer.* Hillsdale, NJ: Lawrence Erlbaum Associates, 1991.

Beitz, Charles. *Political Theory and International Relations.* Princeton: Princeton University Press, 1979.

Benhabib, Seyla. "Cultural Complexity, Moral Interdependence, and the Global Dialogical Community." In Nussbaum and Glover, *Women, Culture, and Development,* 235–255.

Bhatt, Ela. *We Are Poor But So Many.* New York: Oxford University Press, 2006.

Brandt, Richard. *A Theory of the Good and Right.* Oxford: Clarendon Press, 1979.

Deigh, John. "Liberalism and Freedom." In *Social and Political Philosophy: Contemporary Perspectives,* ed. J. Sterba, 151–161. New York: Routledge, 2001.

Elster, Jon. "Sour Grapes." In Sen and Williams, *Utilitarianism and Beyond,* 219–238.

———. *Sour Grapes: Studies in the Subversion of Rationality.* Cambridge: Cambridge University Press, 1983.

Green, T. H. "Liberal Legislation and the Freedom of Contract." In Harris and Morrow, *T. H. Green,* 194–212.

Hampton, Jean. "Feminist Contractarianism." In *A Mind of One's Own: Feminist Essays on Reason and Objectivity,* 2nd ed., ed. Louise Antony and Charlotte Witt, 337–368. Boulder: Westview, 2002.

Harris, Paul, and John Morrow, eds. *T. H. Green: Lectures on the Principles of Political Obligation and Other Writings.* Cambridge: Cambridge University Press 1986.

Harsanyi, John. "Morality and the Theory of Rational Behavior." In Sen and Williams, *Utilitarianism and Beyond*, 39–62.

Korsgaard, Christine. "Fellow Creatures." *The Tanner Lectures on Human Values*, ed. Grethe B. Peterson, vol. 25/6 (2004): 79–110.

Larmore, Charles. *The Morals of Modernity*. Cambridge: Cambridge University Press, 1996.

Murphy, Liam. *Moral Demands in Ideal Theory*. New York: Oxford University Press, 2000.

Nagel, Thomas. *Equality and Partiality*. New York: Oxford University Press, 1991.

Okin, Susan Moller. "Poverty, Well-Being, and Gender: What Counts, Who's Heard?" *Philosophy and Public Affairs* 31 (2003): 280–316.

Pettit, Philip. *Republicanism: A Theory of Freedom and Government*. New York: Oxford University Press, 1997.

Pogge, Thomas. *Realizing Rawls*. Ithaca, NY: Cornell University Press, 1989.

———. *World Poverty and Human Rights: Cosmopolitan Responsibilities and Reforms*. Cambridge: Polity Press, 2008.

Posner, Eric. "Human Welfare, Not Human Rights." *Columbia Law Review* 108 (2008): 1758–1802.

The Pratichi Education Report: The Delivery of Primary Education, a Study in West Bengal, by the Pratichi Research Team, Kumar Rana, Abdur Rafique, Amrita Sengupta, with Introduction by Amartya Sen, number 1. Delhi: TLM Books, 2002.

Rawls, John. *A Theory of Justice*. Cambridge, MA: Harvard University Press, 1971.

———. *Political Liberalism*, expanded ed. New York: Columbia University Press, 1986.

———. *The Law of Peoples*. Cambridge, MA: Harvard University Press, 1999.

Rose, Kalima. *Where Women Are Leaders: The SEWA Movement in India*. Delhi: Vistaar, 1992.

Rothschild, Emma. *Economic Sentiments: Adam Smith, Condorcet, and the Enlightenment*. Cambridge, MA: Harvard University Press, 2001.

Scanlon, Thomas. "Value, Desire, and the Quality of Life." In Nussbaum and Sen, *The Quality of Life*, 185–200.

———. *What We Owe to Each Other.* Cambridge, MA: Harvard University Press, 1999.

Singer, Peter. "Famine, Affluence, and Morality." *Philosophy and Public Affairs* 1 (1972): 229–244.

Stiglitz, J. E., Amartya Sen, J.-P. Fitoussi, et al. *Report of the Commission on the Measurement of Economic Performance and Social Progress.* Online, 2010.

Sunstein, Cass R. *The Second Bill of Rights: F. D. R.'s Unfinished Revolution and Why We Need It More Than Ever.* New York: Basic, 2004.

Unger, Peter. *Living High and Letting Die: Our Illusion of Influence.* New York: Oxford University Press, 1996.

Williams, Bernard. "A Critique of Utilitarianism." In *Utilitarianism: For and Against,* ed. J. J. C. Smart and Bernard Williams, 77–150. Cambridge: Cambridge University Press, 1973.

Acknowledgments

The ideas in this book grew out of my work on the Capabilities Approach over the years. So I really owe thanks to everyone who has given me comments and suggestions on all of this work. But the idea of writing a small book for a general audience as an introduction to the approach grew out of the annual meeting of the HDCA in New Delhi, India, in September 2008. There I gave a preconference lecture to introduce people new to the association to the development of the approach, its varieties, and its challenges. Afterward many people said to me, "You know, if you only sat down and wrote out what you just said here, it would be so useful to us in teaching and in our relations with the general public." I had heard such demands before, but this time I had to admit that it was my responsibility to respond. So I am grateful to everyone who raised that issue at the meeting. As always, I am also grateful to Bina Agarwal, Sabina Alkire, Kaushik Basu, David Crocker, Enrica Chiappero-Martinetti, Flavio Comim, Reiko Gotoh, Mozaffar Qizilbash, Henry Richardson, Ingrid Robeyns, and the other members of the association's "worker bee" group and its rotating executive committee for their amazing efforts and achievements, which have kept the work we are doing before the eyes of the world, and of younger scholars, in a way that nothing short of passionate dedication could. It was out of gratitude for their work that I concluded I owed them the book they want, and I hope I have produced something useful. I am equally grateful to my colleagues at the University of Chicago Law School for their generous engagement with my work. For helpful comments on a draft I am particularly grateful to Daniel Abebe, Emily Buss, Rosalind Dixon, Mary Anne Franks, Tom Ginsburg, Adam Hosein, Jae Lee, Saul Levmore, Richard McAdams, Eric Posner, Lior Strahilevitz, Julie Suk, and David Weisbach. Henry Richardson asked to be identified to me as the author of some wonderful comments given to the Harvard University Press, as did David Crocker for similarly high-value comments, so I owe them both—and an anonymous reader—particular thanks. Naturally, my gratitude to Amartya Sen is fundamental, but since it is evident throughout the book, I need say no more.

INDEX